RAMBLINGS AND RHYME

by Kay Brothers

Copyright©Kay Brothers 2020

All rights reserved

ISBN 978-0-6486579-2-7
Printing 2020
Historic photos from family collections unless otherwise marked.
Illustrations - Mika Miyake
Editor and publisher – Dana McCown

StoryBridge Press
Brisbane, Queensland, Australia
2020

All profits from this book are to be donated to Parkinson's Queensland Inc.

Front Cover design by Mika Miyake

TABLE OF CONTENTS

Friends 7 - 24
Lammie Drive	7
Bird on a Wing	7
Hugging	8
Involvement	9
Book Club	10
Sunflowers	12
Was it You	13
A Guest for Dinner	13
Top of the Mount	14
A Friend	17
Backdrop of Night	17
We'll hold a Word	18
Courage	20
To Joyce	22
Chance Enc. + Tiff	24

Family 25 - 46
Moments	26
Grandma's Lace	27
My Son	29
Merry's 40th	30
Fishing With Dad	31
Uncle Johnny	32
Mother's Day	34
Telling Stories	36
Light a Candle	38
New Babe	39
Aging Gracefully	40
The Family Cat	42
Letter to my Children	42
Colour My World	43
School Bags	44

Humour 47 - 65
Ode to Nippon Loo	47
Finding a Word	47
Packing for UK	48
Steam Train	50
Max	52
Flying Pigs	53
Space Mouse	54
Surprise	56
Work Bug	57
Another Birthday	58
Stuff Bug	60
Tango	62
The Bedroom Clock	63
My Husband's Ear	64
The Hat	66

Nature 69 - 84
Reflections by Sea	69
Magic	70
Renewal	71
Summer Tarry	72
Pelicans	73
Trees, Bush Fires	74
Before the Storm	75
My River	76
Noosa River	78
Reflections River	80
Glory of God	82
Underwater Delight	83
A Blaze of Colour	83
Riding the Wind	84
The Pine	85
New Beginnings	86
Thoughts	86

Old Age 87 - 100
Memories	87
Old Age	88
Mischievous Imp	90
Troublesome Imp	92
A Foreign Land	94
Growing Old	96
The Fox	98

Yesterday	100	Prayer for Refugees	140
The Carnival is Over	102	We have a Problem	142
Talking to God 103 - 118		Homeless	144
Trapped, Thought	103	Meals on Wheels	145
Bend to my Will	104	Drinks Too Much	146
New Years Day	105	**Reflections 147-163**	
Tears in a Bottle	106	Feelings	147
World of Symbols	107	Sit and Reflect	147
Darkness to Light	108	I Want to be Free	148
Saving Grace	109	Nostalgia	149
Role Play	109	Who would a Poet be?	150
Masks	110	Use Time to Reflect	151
Wandering Thought	111	Thought Another Day	151
A Prayer	111	Poet Rumi	152
We'll Plant a Seed	112	My Gift to You	153
Talking to God	113	High above Clouds	153
Gratitude	114	Seize the Day	154
My Cup of Blessings	115	The Fledgling	155
Amazing	116	Light in Window	156
Where are you Lord	118	Little pieces of Light	157
Church Seasons - 121-136		Broken Pieces	158
Christmas Tree	121	Carnival Clown	159
The Wiseman	122	The Great I Am	160
Good Friday People	124	The Silent Times	162
The Spirit	126	Afternoon Reflections	163
Pentecost	127	**Ramblings 164 - 206**	
Christmas Eve	128	Surrogacy Ramblings	164
Christmas 2013	129	Isolation Ramblings	165
The Lone Shepherd	130	Ponderings - Refugees	167
The Christmas Candle	132	Meanderings	170
Pentecost Sunday	133	Year of Grandmother	172
The Wind	133	Friends Ramblings	180
Easter Morn Noosa	135	Light Ramblings	182
Christmas 1980	136	Palm Sunday Ramblings	184
Social Justice - 137-145			
Prayer for Justice	137	Parkinson's One	185
Poem to Kay	138	Parkinson's Two	198
Peppa Pig	138		

INTRODUCTION

This little book began about 40 years ago, when as my husband tells me, I was just "a young chick," and I guess I was! It was a time in our life, which was filled with young children (we had four) and a constant round of chauffeuring kids in four different directions after school.

There was tennis, music lessons, gym - just to name a few, as well as fitting in my own various interests. Those years have long since gone, however during that time, I would put pen to paper and scribble a few verses. The books containing them were consigned to a bottom drawer where they sat for quite some years. During the intervening years, I have written various bits and pieces, which are little ramblings of feelings about my life and circumstances.

Sixteen years ago, I was diagnosed with PD (Parkinson's disease), and my little ramblings became somewhat more focused. I am now 80 years old - no longer a "young chick." Although if you speak to most folk of a comparable age, they will tell you that their bodies may reflect their years, but their minds still remain in that youthful time warp. Sadly it is the mirror, which tells us otherwise!

This little collection of verse and prose is written for my children(4) and grandchildren(8). It would probably still be sitting in the bottom drawer but for the kindness of our friend Dana, whose ability and skill seem to be limitless. I can remember when my own mother died very unexpectedly, I was desperate to find anything that she had written, and I searched through her bible and other bits and pieces and could only find her recipe book. Anything at that time was a comfort.

Years ago my brother gave me a framed piece of calligraphy which features a very pretty bird singing. The verse beside it says, "If you keep a green bough in your heart, a singing bird will come." This hangs in our hallway and I walk past it each time I go in and out. I have always loved this verse. It speaks to me of hope - my singing bird is hope. Yours may be something different, however within my heart lies the seed of hope, which I try to nurture daily. Sometimes I don't quite make it and the green bough becomes a little brown. However this is not for long as I think we all realise that in the tough times, when life seem awry, it is to hope that we cling. Faith and hope together can really sustain us. A friend once gave me a card, which also features a singing bird, which apparently is a Scandinavian proverb defining faith. It says

"Faith is the bird that sings in the darkness before the dawn breaks."

Many times we all sing in the darkness of life knowing that the dawn will surely come.

Kay

1. Pencil sketch of Kay by granddaughter Chloe (16 yrs.)

Friends

THE "LAMMIE DRIVE"

It's fast become a custom, the "lammie drive " each year.
We all assemble apron clad and get ourselves in gear.
Long trestles are erected and stacked with wire trays.
Great bowls of runny chocolate, to dip them in they say!

My neighbour stands beside me, her sleeves rolled up so high
Roll them in the coconut she calls, then leave them there to dry.
We dip and squeeze and squash, it's fun at first, Oh! Gosh.
Then I feel I want to sneeze, my nose begins to itch
However can I scratch it with arms dipped deep in chocolate rich?

We talk and laugh, the day has flown,
In time so short, a pile of "lammies" we have grown
We stack and clean and hose of course.
We all pitch in there's nothing like full force
And so another year of "lammie" drive is o'er
But wait and see, it's safe to say we'll all be back for more.

BIRD ON A WING

As a bird on the wing I would soar
To Heights yet still unknown.
But what would be the use
If I were there alone.

HUGGING

Do you like to hug?
It is therapy you know
It's like the laughter yoga
It leaves you all aglow!

Some folk are not too big on hugs
In fact they're quite bereft
It is a good idea to share
We always have some left!

So bring them out today
If you have some lurking
There is always someone there to welcome
Perhaps they could be hurting!

A hug can speak a thousand words
It says, "You are enough"
You don't have to strive to impress
It does away with all that "stuff."

It reinforces that you count
In a special way
Even the whiskery hairy hugs
Will brighten up your day.

Some folk are into hugging
While others stand aside.
Don't be shy, Make the first move
You'll love it once you've tried.

This troubled world of ours
It might help to free
Perhaps we might discover
That this could be the key?

It can break the barriers that we erect
With just a single act
Our world needs lots of huggers
This surely is a fact!

So come on huggers, set the stage
Practise every day
Big bear hugs are all the go
We can show the way!

INVOLVEMENT

Involvement is a frightening word
To many of us today
Always on the defensive
Ready to shy away
Not willing to count the cost
Have you ever thought
How many are aimlessly lost?

THE BOOK CLUB

In the early days we gathered
Amid our hopes and dreams,
The glow of youth upon us
A wrinkle never seen.

The hours full of chatter
As we shared our love of life,
We cared for our young children,
And coped with all their strife.

We helped each other find
Time to have a break.
It may have been a dinner
Or a movie we would take.

In time there grew a bond
Of care and mutual trust
Our meetings were so special,
In fact they were a must,

We set aside a time
To socialise and eat,
To enjoy each other's company
'Twas a happy way to meet.

Our culinary skills improved
As each month would come around,
Recipes galore
Were always to be found.

The time flew by
And soon an empty nest.
Our life had changed somewhat
But we were full of zest.

A little older
A wrinkle here and there,
Grey hair succumbed to rinses
We didn't really care.

Our love of life not dimmed
Age was not a foe.
Within we still could feel
The child of long ago.

"We need to re-invent ourselves"
Was the decisive cry.
So was born a book club
Best sellers we would buy.

If you come to join us
It may be quite a shock
It could be hard to find
What book we have in stock!

For our discussion ranges
From politics to sex,
Jokes are told with gusto
And no one has an ex!

I must confess at times
Our books may get short shrift.
Does it really matter?
Listening is our gift.

So if you come to visit
A critique great to find,
You may be disappointed
It's not what's on our mind.

Perhaps we'd call it therapy
And we're not ashamed of this.
Live on our little book group
Your presence we would miss.

SUNFLOWERS

The sun at noon shines brightly
Upon your upturned face
Your golden head nods gently
As the breeze your petals grace.

You are but one of many
In a field of golden hue.
Some say your smile is special
I wonder if that's true?

Perhaps in the eye of the beholder
This magic can be seen.
To many, you are all the same,
A mass of gold and green.

Is this a metaphor
Of life and those we meet?
We may share much in common
All that we may greet.

Take time to find the special part
In those whose path we cross.
Don't dismiss them out of hand
Just get beyond the dross.

For underneath there may be
A diamond shining bright.
Give it a chance to sparkle,
It may really need the light.

Too often in our busy world
Obsessed with me and mine
We merely skim the surface
And give so little time!

I will take this little thought
Plant it within my heart
Hoping I will see the harvest,
As in faith I play my part.

WAS IT YOU?

At the foot of the steepest mountain
I found a friend to help me climb.
Was it you?

A GUEST FOR DINER

Recipes galore!
And yet I gather more.

When someone comes to dine
A frantic flurry then is mine.

I nimbly flick through a glossy book
Something exotic for to cook.

Can you guess? I'm about to tell,
I come right back to that dish I know well.

THE TOP OF THE MOUNT

I want to climb
To the top of the mount
I want to drink
From life's great fount.
I need to find
My purpose here
Will you banish
All my fear?

Will you walk
The road I walk
Will you help me
Talk the talk?
Without a friend
I cannot do
This is my plea
I'm asking you?

I'm lonely
And I'm sad
Somehow my life
It seems I've had,
Can I trust you
To come beside?
Will you help me
Turn the tide?

Each day that dawns
I'm all alone,
Heavy of heart
I feel like stone.
I've reached the depths
I know not why.
Please teach me how
I want to fly!

Fly to the heights
That once were mine,
Before this coldness
Became the sign
Of life that feels
It's lost its way
Can you help?
What will you say?

When you see me
In the street,
My pain I hide as
I stop and greet.
Do not be fooled
By what is there
You cannot see
My soul is bare!

I need a friend
To take my hand
To guide me through
This foreign land
To hear the words
I cannot speak
Are you the one I seek?

It is not pity
That I need
Rather someone
Who will lead
Until my steps
Find solid ground
'Til once again
Myself I've found.

I've wandered
Far too long
Missing life's
Great happy song.
I long to join
The joyful fray
Together we'll dance
And share a new day.

So heed my plea
Please throw me a rope
To life help me cling
Fill me with hope
For now I will lift
My sights to above.
Accept me now
Show me your love!

2. Friends old and new at Kay's 80th Birthday Party

A FRIEND

To find myself I moved away
Sweet solitude to seek.
I found a place my head to lay
A haven for my grief.

And in that place there came to me
A friend who sensed my need,
She took my hand in tenderness
I trusted her to lead.

We climbed together a mountain high
Our steps tho' two yet one.
I felt the love that flowed between
Its warmth as the morning sun.

We reached the peak I felt the balm
Of healing in my soul
My heart cried out in joy a psalm of thanks
Again I was whole.

We were never meant to go alone,
Our pain in solitude bear
So let's not reject the love of another
When our heartbreak she offers to share.

THE BACKDROP OF NIGHT

Against the backdrop of night
I saw the moon
The stars so bright
I felt your love
So warm, so true
And I thanked God for someone like you.

WE'LL HOLD A WORD TOGETHER

We'll hold a word together
You and I,
It will be a celebration
To help each other fly.

A word that will be able
To face what life will bring
Binding us as one.
As through our life we wing.

Letters of joy are dancing
Before your lovely face
Each one goes to make the whole.
It is a thing of grace!

This word is really needed
In our hurting world today
If we could only grasp it,
It would help to show the way.

It isn't always easy to
This little word embrace,
It often means there are
Issues we really need to face!

No matter how bleak,
The future seems to be
Take heart this word can
Surely set us free.

A word for all times
Don't dismiss it with a glance
Take it on board,
To help give it a chance.

Our hurting world is crying
It needs to hear this song
Without it we are lost
Our lives will seem all wrong!

It helps to share this word
With someone of same ilk
For they will have the empathy
And will not your courage milk!

Hold it before you every day,
Give thanks for it each morn,
Each hour will be brighter
You will not dread the dawn.

Your spirit will reach out
To share, and lift the load
With others who are walking
Along this rocky road.

What is this word together
Which is a gift so rare?
It's only small I do admit
However we need to share.

And so my friend that precious
Word ...is HOPE.
Hold fast to it forever,
And it will help us cope.

Do not be discouraged
By those who would disdain,
Remember for those who overcome
Life will be a sweet refrain.

COURAGE

Today I shed a tear
Then I heard your voice
Take courage dear heart
I'll help you to rejoice!

Open wide your eyes
To what I've given you
There is much to make you happy
Tho' some things you may rue.

I've given you friends
To help you along the way.
They are my hands and feet
To help you live life's fray.

I've carefully chosen
Those who'll walk beside
Forever they'll be there
When you are in full stride.

I will never leave you
To battle on your own,
You are my child of promise
These words I've carefully sown.

I'll love you unconditionally
Until the end of time
So dear child your spirits lift
I'll make your burdens mine...

When you feel your courage ebbing,
And you are really down,
I'll be there to be your comfort
And ease your troubled frown.

Don't try to do it on your own,
Like many others do,
Just reach out and take my hand
I'll be waiting there for you.

You are my child, my very own
In whom I do delight
I give to you my Kingdom
It is your Royal right.

If you lose your way
Like the Shepherd I will go
I will search for you forever
Just remember this is so.

I have written you forever
On the palm of my hand
Each hair on your head is numbered
Please say you understand.

So dear child you're precious
My gift I will impart
Just heed this little message
Take courage my dear heart!

THOUGHTS

What lies behind us and what lies before us,
Are tiny matters to what lies within us.

TO JOYCE

I pen this little ditty
To you my friend afar.
Our world as one is crying
Tears its beauty mar.

We think of you as we sit
With our memories alone
Reliving all the happy hours
We spent here in this home.

For many years we gathered
To share a week of fun
We were in our later years
In our hearts we were young.

Sometimes we sat and reminisced
Recalling past delights
Other times quite active
As we visited local sights.

We met up with friends to lunch
And socialise.
We celebrated birthdays
Cards and books were our surprise.

Until the time came when that
Wicked imp a memory did steal.
And come what may he held it tight
We could not with him deal.

And so with sadness we saw
What you were working through
We bade you both Godspeed
Home was calling you.

And now we have been plunged
Into a world of real despair
We feel the fear of the unknown
As we try to practise care.

For you my friend it is
An extra load,
Not only is that imp still there
You walk another road.

However this road is shared by many.
It is a broad highway.
To practise being distant
Is not as easy as they say.

If only we could find
A way to stem the tide
To banish this evil virus,
We would no longer need to hide.

The road ahead looks bleak,
We search in vain for hope
We must believe it's there.
'Tis the lifeline that helps us cope.

So dear friend we miss you
And for you we pray.
Fight that imp with courage
Each morn heralds a new day.

CHANCE ENCOUNTERS

Some are unhappy these
Meetings by chance!
Others we wish we could
Make merry and dance.

Many a friendship
Started this way.
I have several
Which last to this day.

To meet and to feel,
You've found someone who's real.
In common you share,
Soon souls you can bare!

Friendships so happy,
Such pleasures are mine
With folk who are special
Our paths will entwine!

A TIFF....

What would happen if you and I
Should have a tiff?
Would you come and talk to me
Or would you unforgiving be?

FAMILY

\# 3. Russell and Kay at the Birthday Party

\# 4. All of Kay's Grandchildren at the party.

MOMENTS

To capture a moment
As it slips from your grasp
Gently reach out
In your hand firmly clasp.

Times that are special...
Elusive they are
Can vanish forever
Life flings them afar.

Moments so fleeting,
Have slipped through our hand
They've stolen away
As the tide on the sand.

Can we secrete them
In boxes of gold
Like jewels they are precious.
To have and to hold!

Times with our family
With sweet repartee
We cannot replace them
I think you'll agree.

Moments of beauty,
To have and enfold
A memory awakening
A joy to behold!

The hours of friendship
Of great reverie
Moments so special
We plainly do see.

Those special times hold
In your hand tight
Nurture them carefully.
Or they will take flight.

Snapshots of life
Now play through our mind
Each moment can help us
Our happiness find.

When life is closing
And we look to our past
These reflections on life
Surely will last.

GRANDMA'S LACE

It hangs upon the bedpost
And gives a certain grace
The threads now thin and worn
I call it Grandma's lace.
The years have passed and I am unsure
From whence it really came
I know there is a story
A tapestry to frame.

I lie in bed and ponder
And imagine sights it's seen.
Lives it has been part of
The good years and the lean.
Another time, another life
A century ago
Was it a fancy pillow sham
Or perhaps a lacy throw?

Tonight I sense the romance
In the beauty of the lace.
Has it been a gift of love
To follow an embrace.
Was it a handsome soldier
Who stole my grandma's heart
And the war to end all wars
That kept them far apart.

I wish dear grandma
As you laid your head to rest
That you could have looked across the years
And see how you've been blest
For God has given you
A family most fair
They think of you with love
And are grateful for your care.

Now I am a grandma
And often do recall
The times we spent together
Happy memories still enthral.
For the little girl
Who played happily by your side,
Life has come full circle
I take your place with pride.

Happy thoughts have bidden
Memories new and old
Some are tinged with silver
More often they are gold.
So as I dim the light
A smile upon my face
I give thanks that on the bedpost
Hangs my Grandma's lace.

MY SON

A little lie to me you told
With confidence you spoke
Your tale so blithe and bold.

Perhaps your tender age
Just could not see
The inconsistencies
That glared right out at me.

To your story
You held so fast
I wondered how long
This pretence would last.

I knew that soon
I would learn the truth
Sadly I looked
On my stubborn youth.

Do not practise to deceive
For then from others
Little respect
You'll receive.

Oh! My son,
When will you learn
That earnest truth
True trust will earn!

MERRY'S 40TH BIRTHDAY

Merry you're the big 40.
Lift your spirits, don't feel low.

Embrace the hours of each new day
Welcome all that comes your way.

Life brings many precious gifts
Unwrap them all and through them sift.

At times you may feel some surprise
When a gift comes in disguise.

For life is all not froth and bubble
Perhaps we face a bit of trouble.

And all is not just light of heart
But in life's school it plays a part.

Sorrow and joy are close, close friends
They're with us till our journey ends.

Today we bring you blessings real
And pray God's peace across you steal.

We'll sing and dance and cut the cake
Come one and all, WE'LL CELEBRATE.

FISHING WITH DAD

I'll catch a little fish said he
As off he set with dad and me!

On his shoulder slung the line and bait
While waiting at home an empty plate.

On the riverbank together we sat
Soon to be joined by the family cat.

He cast his line in but a flash
Swiftly it went with a really loud splash.

The sun was warm our shirts we shed
Before we knew it our noses all red.

I boiled the Billy and passed the mug
Then young Bobbie felt his line give a tug.

He pulled on his reel and cried in glee
For sure it was a fish he could see.

Now he jerked his rod as quickly he wound
We held our breath there was hardly a sound.

It came to the surface what a thrill
Soon unhooked it was lying still.

He turned away
Alas! Alack!
Suddenly we saw the cat
Licking his lips... where the fish had sat!

UNCLE JOHNNY

Of Uncle Johnny I have
Memories fair.
I oft giggle when
Thoughts go there.

He was my nana's brother
He lived his life unwed
In later life he came to her
Was given board and fed.

Of his early life, little did I know.
Across the table he'd wink at me
As into his dinner he tucked
I'd laugh in childish glee.

The night that stands out
In my memory clear
Was the nights we had fish
This meal to his heart was dear.

As much as he loved it
Of a bone he was scared.
Strange as his family
On fish had been reared!

Each time it was served
Nana was there,
Chunks of bread in her hand
A great slap on the back
To get him on track.

This performance was part
Of so many a meal
His panic no doubt
Was scary and real.

To this day when
Fish we are eating
This memory comes
From the past it's a greeting.

Whenever it is served
As much as I love fish
I cannot help but see Johnny
There surveying his dish.

But who am I to talk
I also am a bone freak,
I pick through my meal
As gold I would seek!

It's strange how memories
Come to the fore,
They come unbidden
There are many more!

They're contagious they
Tumble across one's mind,
A box filled with treasure
Which is ours to find!

MOTHERS' DAY!

Mothers' day is special,
It comes but once a year,
We gather with each other,
And mothers' virtues hear.

All niggles are forgotten,
There's a spirit of good will
For this day at least
We will together feast!

Mum has become a Saint,
She's toasted and adored,
Forgotten are the grievances
Problems we have stored.

Tomorrow is another day,
Will we then affirm
The happy words we've spoken
To what will we return?

Mothers are not Saints,
Tho' special they may be,
At times they too have feet of clay,
With this you will agree!

They make mistakes,
They wish their lips to seal
When thoughtless words they utter
Become so slow to heal!

They often walk on eggshells,
Unsure of how to act,
Especially with their adult child
Indeed this is a fact!

Some have another generation
Who join them on this day,
A full circle they have come.
Now they can have their say.

Gran can be a hero
In their still unopened eyes,
They see her in a different light
For her they'll stand and fight!

Many things are written
About mums that aren't quite true,
Sometimes a little mawkish
But these are just a few!

Mothers are not saints
Their children are on loan
They need to see
That seeds of love are sown!

Sadly there are mothers,
Who will not be seen this day.
Their way they've lost,
For them we need to pray!

Mothers deserve each accolade
That comes along their way
We wish them joy and happiness
As they celebrate today.

From Mother Theresa...
"Kind words can be short and easy to speak, but their echoes are truly endless."

TELLING STORIES

We have a story to tell
Our lives a book
Open the cover
Lets take a look.

Turn the page
And what do we see?
Our tales will be different
You and me!

Our childhood
Happy and free
Or is it sadness
That we see?

Perhaps the years
That came between
Were fraught with worry
As we became teen!

Our vocation in life
Ours to choose
We are unique
We walk in our shoes!

Time will slip by
With much to recall
Year after year we're
Held in its thrall.

Then the time comes
Of another grace
We suddenly find
The lines on our face.

Yes! We've grown old
We can hardly believe
The face in the mirror
Looking we grieve.

Grief is short lived.
We look down the years
Happiness there
And always some tears.

No matter what comes
We've charted our course.
Life it is called
With little remorse.

Strewn over time
Our memories dance
We each have our own
Some wrapped in romance.

Now is the time
To smell all the flowers
Nostalgia is great
It rolls back the hours.

We can sit and reflect
Tell our story unique
Open the page
We can all take a peek!!

TODAY I LIGHT A CANDLE

Written on June 29, 2006. The day after my father died.

We were in Sienna, Italy.
We went to the cathedral there where I lit a candle for him.

Today I light a candle
A symbol of new life
At first it's just a flicker
And now it's burning bright.

Today I light a candle
It is for you and me
Joy and sadness mingle
I know your soul is free.

Today I light a candle
To share across the years
Bringing happy memories
And drying every tear.

Today I light a candle
For the birthday we have missed.
God took you by the hand
And your spirit gently kissed.

Today I light a candle
To make your journey bright
You've run your race dear dad
You're living in the light.

NEW BABE

To welcome a new babe into the family. (for the grandparents)

Great delight! Oh! What joy!
Perhaps a girl? If not a boy.
It does not really matter what the sex will be
For you're both to be a "Grandy"
A blessing you'll agree.

Your peace to be invaded
By a little dynamo
You will love this little tot
What promise he will sow.

You will join the happy throng
Of those who love to boast.
Who snap a million photos
So their "littlie" they can toast.

With high chairs, cots and teddies
Your home will over-run
New found skills will come your way
Learning will be fun.

Your writing will soon become
With a "Grandy's" wise insight
In the book of family history
A new page you will write.

The road you walk is changing.
You will find a new direction
So enjoy this special time
Use it for much reflection.

AGEING GRACEFULLY

My husband has a ponytail
It really is quite cute.
Can you imagine all the comments?
It sure is bearing fruit!

He is not young.
I guess he is quite old,
Although he does not feel it.
Tis' now the time called Gold!

On top his hair is rather sparse,
Curls gently grace his neck.
I say! Exploit! What you have got.
Don't worry! What the heck!

If you have reached this age
You, eccentric now can be.
Inhibitions you have shed
Have fun and just feel free.

Perhaps there will be more
A "tat" might be the go?
What a stir that would cause
My thoughts race to and fro.

A diamond stud to grace the ear
Could also be a thought.
Who says that when we're old,
We cannot, or we ought?

At first it was a joke
All a bit of fun.
Now I think he's bitten
With it he's on the run!

As the years fly by
And we have reached this stage
It isn't very easy,
For us to have a rage.

We have not lost our spirit
Tho' our bodies are not sleek,
Our capacity for fun
Is still up near the peak!

To grow old gracefully
It does not mean we're staid.
Perhaps it shows the "stuff"
Of what we're really made.

When you get there.
You'll know just what I mean,
Your love for life will double
As you see the years grow lean.

So each day when we awake
A new day we will greet,
We will welcome every challenge
It head on will we meet.

So back to where we started
About a pony tail
Even if you feel a tad extreme
Don't worry you'll not fail.

Just ignore the folk that frown
Don't worry if they mutter
Feel good about yourself
You know you're not a "nutter."

We may be rich in years
But still there is much more
So start to feel excited
Who knows what is in store?

THE FAMILY CAT

BLACK AS INK

What would you think
If in the night
You saw shining bright
Two eyes of green
With little else to be seen?
They gleam and glitter
You feel all a-twitter
They move Oh! So near
Your hands shake with fright
You reach for the light
To find on the mat
Your favourite cat!!

LETTER TO MY CHILDREN.

My children - One day

You also a parent will be
So please remember something for me.
First of all just bear in mind
We have always tried to be loving and kind.
So when at times you have a date.
Tell us where and if you'll be late.

Perhaps you think there is no need
To bother you with all this screed.
And so although you feel we fuss
Please just try to think of us
For one day you too, no doubt
Will know what we "were on about."

COLOUR MY WORLD

(Thinking of Dad and his increasing age)

Old age is a colour I've recently found,
It's not red or yellow
Or something profound.

Its shades are more sombre
They're grey and they're sad
Especially for you if it's your elderly dad.

It's not even tinged with
Silver or gold
Instead it's quite stark a pain to behold.

Youth is a colour
It dazzles with light
Vibrant in hue all happy and bright.

The shades of midlife
Are mine to recall
A colourful mix to help us stand tall.

At times in our life
The shades bring change
From sadness to joy the colours will range.

Be it reds or purples
Blacks or greys
The colours of life will weave though our days.

SCHOOL BAGS

Will it always be our lot
To trip on school bags
Placed in just the spot
To cause a traffic jam
And tempers running hot.
Uneaten lunches tucked away
For what purpose one could say
I guess it's part of life so short,
Just give me patience to do as I ought.

5. Family times.

MORE BROTHERS' CLAN

#6. Mika, Angelina and David.

#7. Portrait artist Chloe with father Andrew, who lives in Hong Kong.

8. Granddaughter Angelina and her partner Sean.

9. Kay and Russell at the start of their life's adventure together.

HUMOUR

ODE TO NIPPON LOO

Now in Japan we're here, we're there.
So to that room we oft repair!

How amazing, how divine
For there to be a haven fine.

It sprays, it cleans, it warms the bot.
The first I've found to do the lot!

FINDING A WORD TO RHYME WITH ORANGE

If it was red,
Yellow or blue
How easy it is a rhyme to pursue.

Or if we say lime, lemon or apple
Much easier for us to grapple.

If it's a town try Seymour or Burke
Lots of words around them do work.

For a poet looks always his word skill to share
Rhyme or prose we don't really care.

PACKING FOR OUR UK TRIP

I'm just about to pack
We're on the move again
The bag is sitting waiting
It's driving me insane.

Will I take my tights
And throw in a top or two?
Should I take my evening shoes?
I'm teetering to and fro!

Every year it is the same,
This dilemma always mine.
The bag is packed not once
But "just one more time."

Clothes are strewn across the room
You can almost hear me sigh!
I'm looking to the heavens
Perhaps there's help on high!

But no, I'm left to struggle,
With what I need to pack
How many books to read?
I'm eyeing off my stack!!

And then there's medication
Gone are the days of travel light.
The pills are carefully counted
We need to get this right.

At last it seems I'm done!
I think I've managed well
When from the bedroom
There comes a mighty yell.

I hear my husband's irate tone
As to his side I speed.
I need a good excuse
My innocence I plead.

Surely it is feasible
For me to pinch some space.
Males do not need the dress
For all the outings we may face.

Sweet talking sometimes works,
These times it's gold I've struck.
He's taking less, and buying more
It seems we're both in luck!

I'll be glad when our feet
Upon the U.K soil we place.
The flight will be behind us
Our friendships we will grace.

So dear Lord bless us
Again from home away,
We ask for travelling mercies
On this our holiday.

OUR STEAM TRAIN ADVENTURE

It was dark when we awoke
We faced an early start,
Our infectious zeal, propelling us.
We were loath to miss a part!

Where were we going?
You well may ask?
To be dressed at this hour
Is no mean task.

Well a taste of nostalgia
Was driving our intent.
A trip upon a steam train
Somehow momentum lent.

To reach Toowoomba was our goal,
Some four hours was the plan
Little did we know
This train was not "the Ghan."

We reached the bottom of the range
All was going well!
We had had some cheese and "bikkies"
Our appetites to quell.

The diesel then attached itself
To pull us up the hill,
Then the trouble surfaced
It did not fit the bill!
We huffed and puffed,
All to no avail,
In Warwick a replacement found
Its progress like snail mail!

So for some hours we sat
Thinking of ways to fill our time,
And then our lovely Sheryl.
Made a suggestion quite sublime.

I jest of course (about sublime)
She asked us all to stand,
And laughter yoga was the mime!

The others in the carriage,
Looked on with happy smile
I think they thought us crazy,
Until one we seemed to rile!

She objected to our goings on,
We were noisy, could we stop?
Chastened we took our seats
At times the flak we have to cop.

However this little exercise
Had cheered us up no end
Try laughing like a kookaburra,
And see how your spirits mend!

Soon we were on our way,
Eight hours did we spend,
Our aim to see some gardens,
Fast coming to an end.

However, all was not lost
At the Carnival of Flowers,
The wonderful prize garden
Lilies and fairy bowers!

We did not eat a meal at any time
But snacked on this and that.
The homeward journey found us
Napping as we sat.

However all came alive,
When two bottles were produced,
There's nothing like a red and white.
Our weariness was soon reduced!

And so we turned at midnight
Our steps to home once more,
Our desire for nostalgia,
Left in the land of yore.

MAX   (OUR MISCHIEVOUS GERMAN SHEPHERD)

He's done it again, alas and alack!
What else can I do but give him a smack.
He jumps and he prances no remorse does he show.
He thinks it's a game like the ball that I throw.

How can I teach him on the line it must stay?
My sheets he will swing on for half of the day.
I rant...and I rave...for my patience he'll tax
Can I give him away my puppy dog Max?

FLYING PIGS

This was written to encourage you to take heart when to a comment made by you, is greeted with that old saying, " Pigs might fly."

Do you know that Pigs can fly?
Perhaps like me you wonder why
When others put our words to scorn.
Spirits drop we feel forlorn.

A turn of phrase by others used.
Sometimes leaves us quite abused
So when you're told that "Pigs might Fly"
Do not even blink an eye.

I have a pig who lives with me
His eyes have yet the ground to see
He flies on high with nary a care
I only need to see him there.

He helps me keep my head held high
How glad I am that " Pigs can fly."

THE SPACE MOUSE

He's white with green antlers
With knobs on the end
He lives in my house
He's become my dear friend.

He's a funny shape
Perhaps you'd say
To me he's cute
I love him that way.

I met him last week
In the garden green
The strangest thing
I've ever seen.

I sat beside him.
He did not mind.
We found a place
That no one could find.

He told me such stories
Oh! What fun
As we played together
In the morning sun.

I asked him how
He came to be
So far from home
And here with me.

You may think his answer
Strange may seem
He came to earth
On a laser beam.

    His antler knobs
      Are really queer.
    I think they help
      To get him in gear.

    A flick and a twist
      They seem to flash
    He can run so fast
    I'm afraid that He'll crash.

    He told me he lives
      On the point of a star
    I look from my window
      And gaze up afar.

    I found him a shoe box
      To sleep in at night
    I like to think that
      He's tucked up tight.

    He has to be a secret
      For now.
    If my dad found out
      There could be a row.

    You see my mum is afraid
      Of frogs and mice.
    I don't think she'd like him
      Nor would she be nice.

    I took him to school
      Tucked deep in my port.
    I hope by my teacher
      I won't be caught.

I took him to see my friend
Ruff the dog
We sat and we talked
On an old bent log.

I know that one day
Away he will beam.
My adventure will then
Be a far away dream.

SURPRISE! SURPRISE

At last it has happened....
I've entered the fray.
It seems all at once I face a new day!

The devil that once I looked at askance
Is now partnering me
In perennial dance.

With patience and practice
I'm ready to go
In time I will conquer this long time foe.

Have you guessed?
I'll let the name drop
Would you believe it's a new laptop!

THE WORK BUG

I can't recall I've ever seen it
Tho' it's sting I've often felt
Only for it's buzzing
My husband I could melt.

It seems to be elusive
I can never pin it down.
When I quiz my better half
He answers with a frown.

It seems that once you're bitten
There is little you can do.
Its venom is so potent
The family feel it too.

One day I'll find that nuisance bug
Clever though he be
I'll clip his subtle wings
So no longer he'll be free.

Can you imagine what
Life will be like
When no longer that creature
We have to fight?

ANOTHER BIRTHDAY

I've had another birthday,
And lovely as it is,
As well as being fun
It gets me in a tizz!

You see there is no escaping
I am growing old!
I can use creams and potions
In an effort to delay...
But still a wrinkle new.
Greets my every day.

I can exercise and pretend
That my body is still firm
If I'm honest I will tell you
It is not the shape I'd yearn.

Last week I was seduced
As I read the Internet
A magic cream on offer
A free trial I could get.

Religiously I cleansed and
Followed to a T.
My eyes with bags and circles
Alas! Looked back at me.

Ever increasing now
The years are flying by
Where have they gone?
Who stole them is my cry?

Still a young girl is living
Within this body old
You cannot see her
At times she feels quite bold!

At times I feel a shock
With a wayward mirror glance
Is that stranger me,
Or another by some chance?

There is no magic wand
To bring an about face
Alas! The truth is there
I must accept with grace.

However perhaps there are plusses
At which we need to look
We are content in our own skin
Life is an open book.

We have put aside our prejudice
The years have taught us much
We have moved on from rigidity
We have known life's gentle touch.

We can look back with gratitude
On lessons we have learnt
This time of quite reflection
I think we've truly earned.

With fondness we can see
The foibles of our youth
With hindsight comes wisdom
We don't claim to have the truth.

Love is the key to happiness
We practise opening the door
We know what lies beyond
Will lead us on to more!

So now I will embrace
My arms held out to greet
The years that still are mine
I'm happy now to meet.

THE STUFF BUG

A strange malady holds us
We're caught up in its sway
So many of us are bitten
We often lose our way.

There is a greedy little bug
He attacks where there's a will
A respecter of persons he is not
With him we're never still.

He has a clever tongue
He drives us on to more
So cleverly he urges
We have no room to store.

His name is "stuff"!
He is a bug of some repute,
Many of us have felt his bite
Of this there's no dispute.

Once you have encountered him
His power you are in
His wings close all about you
He even bites within.

Before you know
An overflow of bits and bobs,
Where e're you look
Your space he robs.

He loves to see us spend
Or perhaps to just collect,
Remember he's the stuff bug
He loves us to connect.

His venom is so potent.
That bug is never still
We have an overflow
He loves our lives to fill.

Well I have decided
It is time to now be free.
I'll banish him forever.
Difficult it may be.

I'll clip his wings
When he comes a'flying.
It will not happen overnight
Of that there's no denying.

Just think of the delight
When we reclaim our space
That bug has gone
And life again we face.

So if you also suffer
From this thing of "stuff"
Do not be discouraged,
That bug just give a cuff.

Be firm in your resolve.
Don't let him hang around.
Get rid of him forever
Blessings will abound.

THE TANGO

The tango to dance
Is my desire,
To be light on my feet
I do aspire.

This intimate dance
We start with a hug
In a short time,
We're "cutting" a rug!

I'm so glad you're not
A fly on the wall
Even though I do try
To give it my all.

My partner is patient
He needs to be
It takes me awhile
The steps to see.

The music I like
It has a real beat
If only I could learn
Where to place my feet.

It's all very simple
We walk and we turn,
However a gold star
I'm sure I won't earn.

I have a wish to
Take the lead.
Why on earth
Do I have this need?

Perhaps in life
There's a lesson in dance
Take time to be still
That is your chance!

THE BEDROOM CLOCK

TIME PASSES BY INTERMINABLY
SO STILL THE NIGHT
I feel your presence
You with the luminous face
ARCH-ENEMY
IF ONLY YOU WOULD REST
Yet relentlessly you toil
How I long to punish you
And all your plans to foil.

Would you deny me the
Sweet Solace of sleep
Is there a plot
Your vengeance to reap?

ARCH ENEMY
LET ME GO. I'M TIRED OF COUNTING SHEEP!

MY HUSBAND HAD A CRITTER IN HIS EAR

My husband had a critter in his ear.
This was his cry to me.
He swore he heard it chirping
How could we set it free?

Frantically we rifled
Through oils and all that stuff.
I must admit that with his ear
I was a trifle rough!

After much pouring
And shaking of the head
Together with some words of colour
Which were better left unsaid.

He pronounced the critter
Must surely now be dead.
The vexing question now
How to extract the body from his head?

We made a tele call
Our Trusty Doc and friend.
He assured us not to worry
His ear would surely mend.

Home he came
A smile upon his face.
His ear restored or so he thought
'Twas by the doctor's grace.

A month went by of peace
And all was happy and calm
The critter almost forgotten
Lived on in happy yarn.

Alas! Alack the dark clouds
Ready now a storm to whip
My husband in great distress
Calls again, "My ear is limp!"

Yes! That little critter
Resurrected he had been.
My better half is in a flap
With hand to ear he's really green.

The critter's chirp is very loud
Which is really no surprise,
His vocal cords have had a rest
And he is singing a reprise.

My husband now in panic mode
Imagination working overtime!
"What has that little imp been doing,
What mischief has he wrought in this ear of mine?"

With thoughts of this critter
Burrowing deep in his brain
Laying eggs that will scatter
The doc he sees again.

It is tinnitus you have,
So put your mind at rest,
Do away with crazy critters
For your doc knows best.

THE HAT!

If my hat could talk
What would it say?
It is my happy hat,
Its days are never grey!

Life's celebrations its had part
When days are full of fun
It frames my face
And shades me from the sun!

It first enjoyed a wedding
Many years ago
T'was my son's
Indeed a marvelous show!

It was birthed for that occasion.
The years have quickly passed,
Dressed prettily with flowers
Still they seem to last.

That day was a joyous one
Oh! I wish my hat could voice,
The simple pleasures that were ours,
In which we did rejoice.

The little church in which they made
Their promise and their vow,
To cherish and to love
They are still together now.

The flowers that his bride
Gave to me that day
The hallstand do they grace
They take the pride of place.

This is naive this little poem,
Of that I am aware,
Like the paintings of a child
Splashing colour without care.
But care I do, a vehicle is my hat.

To carry you, and share,
Some of my happy times,
Which are dancing here and there.

My hat then went a tripping
Guess where? The Melbourne cup.
I did not travel with it,
A friend wore it for luck.

It has also been so lucky
To enjoy a great high tea,
It hobnobbed along with
Others, its counterparts did see!

And what an array they were,
A sight to dazzle and amaze,
Ribbons, lace and roses.
It left in a great daze!

A garden party was a time
Of colour and of sun,
I wore you then and it was
So much fun.

Tiny sausage rolls and dainty
Bread delights,
You were much admired
People had you in their sight!

The ladies Oohed and Ahhed!
The fellows dipped their lid,
I loved the adoration
Enjoyed it as a kid!

So you see my hat
Has had a happy life,
Not blown by the wind,
Nor worried by strife!

It sits on its hook
A smile on its face.
I'll wear it some more
I know that for sure!

10. Noosa boards on a calm day.

11. Noosa beautiful coastline.

Nature

REFLECTIONS BY THE SEA

The wind was kind today
As it gently tossed the ocean spray
It laughed as it danced on the carpet of foam
And playfully tickled the bird all alone.

The boy on the board smiled in delight
As the breakers appeared...what a welcome sight!
The child on the edge squealed in glee
As the foam swirled around...it was all he could see.

Singing and swaying it teased each wave,
Backwards and forwards like a mischievous knave
I sat on the sand and felt the breeze
As it swept through my hair and caressed the trees.

How pleasant it is to be at the beach
And have all these treasures within your reach.
Savour each moment and hold it tight
A happy memory is yours to delight!

MAGIC

I believe in Magic
Do you?
If you answer yes
We are among the few.

Folk who are blessed
In each moment to see
The dew as a teardrop
Shed by each tree!

The spider who weaves
With gossamer fine
Her web of silk
To show its design.

For those who live in the moment
Tis' magic to see
Who take time to spend
Just learning to be!

Each snowflake that falls
A diamond can be
Transformed by its sparkle
For you and for me.

The sun as it sets,
Wondrous colours unfold
It is God's canvass
What skill to behold!

The moon in the evening
Slung low in the sky
The twinkling of stars
Shedding light from on high.

Soft warmth of the darkness
Like velvet to touch
Sends the message of love
Needed so much.

With eyes open wide
We colour our days
From the moment we rise
To the setting sun's rays.

The seashore is filled
With magic bright,
With tiny sea critters
And shells to delight.

Take time to enjoy
Not forgetting to look
Magic blooms like a flower
In each cranny and nook.

RENEWAL

The gentle shower in spring
Bright colours do a rainbow bring
Small green shoots to greet the earth
Seeds long sown now give birth.

Sweet scent of honey in the air
Bees that buzz 'round blossoms fair
Oh! What joy this brings to you
As nature does her earth renew.

SUMMER WHY DO YOU TARRY

Summer why do you tarry?
Winter has been so long
I weary so of waiting
To hear the new spring song.

Patiently I've sat and watched
The dry fields there
How I long for new green shoots
To greet the earth so bare.

My body yearns for respite
From the rigors of the cold
Gone are the days of youth
And now I'm growing old.

I want to smell again
The fragrance of the spring
I want to see the bright colours
That a change of season bring.

To walk again with pleasure
Down a winding country lane
The winter of my suffering vanished
Along with all the pain.

And so I feel the call
Of life that's ever new
Do not tarry summer
I'm ready now for you.

PELICANS

We have a lonely pelican,
We think he's lost his mate
He swims in our marina.
We ponder on her fate!

Perhaps she's lost her way
In our recent river flood
Or perhaps she thinks her mate
Is somewhat of a dud.

Has she given him the flick,
And found another love.
Could be that she's enjoying
Some ecstasy above!

I guess if we can do it
Pelicans have the right
I wonder whether she will last
Or will she see the light?

He's a rather handsome bird,
Graceful as they come
They all look the same to me
'Tho it's not me having fun.

Lo and behold today I saw
A very happy sight
Two pelicans frolicking
They looked so right.

Are they giving each other
A dose of common sense?
Have they baby chicks somewhere
It could be things are tense.

I hope this works for them,
And together again will be
It's sad to see a lone pelican
Don't you agree?

TREES

Trees are things of beauty
I love them everyone
From the tiny struggling sapling
To the great majestic gum.

Their foliage all so different
As they bloom in early spring
The call of birds forever
From their branches seem to ring.

I can sit in deep reflection
In the gentle spread of shade
They're one of the nicest gifts
Our creator ever made.

THE BUSH FIRE

Fire consumes
Dying embers
Black ash
Stark skyline
Painful pictures
Vivid in my mind
Tomorrow - re-creation.

"A thought to remember: A misty morning often gives way to a glorious day."

THE CALM BEFORE THE STORM

The calm before the storm
How deceptive it can be
You feel that all is well
In one accord you all agree.
And then with fierce momentum
Angry clouds appear.
The roar of thunder fills the air
Our hearts begin to fear.

Bright streaks of lightning dart
Across the darkened sky
The winds begin to howl
A plea for shelter is my cry.
And then the heavens open
Cascades of water flow
The fear within recedes.
Perhaps again I'll grow.

Words of anger fiercely spoken
Make me want to run.
My spirit needs tranquillity,
The warmth of morning sun
And yet I know we all must stand
And weather the storms of life.
We cannot hide ourselves
Forgetting the trouble and strife.

And so each day I'm learning
To accept what comes my way
And slowly now am finding
I cope with more each day.

MY RIVER

On the river where I live
Sparkling jewels are mine.
The sun kissed clouds
At early morn give to me a sign.

A promise of what's in store
Of beauty for this day,
The sun a ball of fire
Soon will be a shining ray.

The river is a lifeblood
For this city of mine.
In and out it ducks and weaves
Never in straight line.

Along its banks are many parks
Children are at play
How I love the river
It gives me pleasure all the day.

We say the ocean has its moods
My river does as well.
At times it can be gentle
With just a tiny swell.

In times of flooding,
It pursues its chosen path.
Relentless it can be
'Tis mighty in its wrath.

A city built upon a river
Offers much I would suspect
For this special river
I have a great respect.

In the early evening hours
I walk along her banks
Ferries sailing up and down
For which the crowd give thanks.

The boats in the Marina
Sitting still at rest
Now come alive as owners
Return to watery nest!

A moonbeam steals across the sky
The fading light gives way
Come play with me she whispers
As she tosses me fine spray.

A lone swan swims in solitude
Has she lost her mate?
She holds herself so gracefully
Not worried for his fate.

As I sit with her this evening
We wait the world's drum roll
I sit with great expectancy
Her magic fills my soul.

12. Brisbane River in front of our home.

NOOSA RIVER

Come walk with me at dusk
Such beauty you will see
Along the Noosa river
It's there for you and me!

The birds are our companions
As they chase each other round
Their raucous voices calling
A cacophony of sound.

Brightly coloured splashes
A flutter of a wing
Kindness of our natural world
What pleasure it does bring!

The pelicans are sailing
With heads held high
Some with flap of wing
Ready now to fly.

Children building sand castles
On a strip of sandy beach
A teen is paddle boarding
Just a little out of reach.

Catching their eye with a smile
A moment I would not miss
Two lovers on a rustic bench
Stealing a happy kiss.

Many folk are walking
Their dogs both large and small
We chat and make new friends
As darkness starts to fall.

A father casts the line
For his fishing eager son
The fish not really biting
But what a lot of fun.

Two young girls are posing
For the camera used by dad
A record of this holiday
Surely must be had.

Aroma from sizzling sausages
On barbecues galore
The gastric juices stirring
Who could ask for more?

Fish and chips and pizza
A glass of good white wine
Families happily picnic
It is a special time.

Soft hues of pastel colour
Now trail across the sky
The sun has bid farewell
The stars will soon be high.

If only a canvass I could paint.
I would capture there for you
The magic of this moment,
So you could share it too!

13. Kay enjoying the Noosa River.

REFLECTIONS FROM THE RIVER

In the cool of the evening
Feeding the ducks
With scraps from our plate
Under the old gum tree
Me and my mate!

The birds clad in colour
Were playing tig,
Winging their way
To their evening gig!

Backwards and forwards,
They dipped and they sang,
Twosomes and threesomes
Their melody rang.

The river was quiet
A small boat now and then
The sun slipped from sight
As I lift my pen.

A whisper of breeze
Arising now
Leaves gently falling
Upon the ground
Sun waving farewell
As it turned around.
Now what has it found?

I wonder on whom it
Will shine,
What they will be doing
At this moment in time?

Will they be rising
To greet a new morn,
Thanking the sun
As a new day is born?

Perhaps they are waking
To a day that is dark,
When life with its problems
No more a lark!
The sun no longer
Will light their way
They kneel and pray
For its healing ray.

When we are content
Do we think of the other
Whose life is in chaos
He could be our brother?
Moments of quiet
Help our spirit discern
New insight to learn.

So take time to reflect,
When sitting at ease
At the fountain of life
We can take our fill
If only we learn to be still.

An autumn leaf
Falls upon the water
Our life drifts by!

THE GLORY OF GOD!

Clinging to each petal
Is early morning dew.
Night's soft blanket tucked away
We greet the day anew.

The sunrise offers colours
Deep pinks and amber gold
We look in awe and wonder
God's canvas to behold.

The miracle of life is ours,
With open arms embrace
Blessed are we
We can this day face.

The noisy chatter of the birds,
As they fly we know not where
They sing to one another
They flit from here to there.

The wonder of each child
Given for us to love
A precious gift is ours
It is from God above.

So welcome our world
Created for you and me
To God be the glory
Forever may it be!

Icicles....crystal clear...suspended in time.
Beauty sublime.

UNDERWATER DELIGHT

Through water crystal clear
I gazed in sheer delight
The ocean bed below
Now magic to my sight.

Soft shades of green and muted pink
The coral soon became
A place to lose myself
And of its beauty drink.

Myriads of tiny fish
Iridescent colours all aglow
Across the ocean bed they swim
In all directions go.

A fairyland of beauty far beneath the sea
A world apart
On which to gaze
Independent of you and me.

A BLAZE OF COLOUR

A blaze of colour greets my day
Bright oranges, pinks and purple
African tulips and crepe myrtle.
Frangipanis, ginger plants
Gums of green from my window seen.

Thank you Lord for colours bright
I love them more than just "black and white"

RIDING ON THE WIND!

I will ride on the wind
I will soar and fly,
I will wave to the birds
As they pass me by
And I'll shout my praise
To the rising sun
As it hides the clouds
On its morning run.

I will dance on its beams
As they light our sky
I'll give thanks to the moon
As it leaves with a sigh.
The star of the morning
I'll wave farewell
She winks at me
And I'm under her spell.

The wind is wild
As along we race
She rattles the leaves
And brings tears to my face
Her passion is boundless
And filled with desire
Is this where we get
Wind, earth and fire.

We dip and we weave,
Through our universe great
I'm wondering just when
Her mood she will sate
I'm one with her
As we race along
Come ride with me
As she sings her song.

At times she is gentle
A breeze to caress
To cool our spirits
And softly refresh.
Now she's a demon
With dread our hearts fill
She is causing much havoc
Why this ill will?

Her head and tail used
To gain speed
Whether we fly in the air
We can trust her to lead
Bringing pleasure to many
She's roaming today
She can harness power
Banishing clouds of grey.

So ride this mighty wind
Come with me
Be filled with her passion
She'll always be free
She'll be here forever
Riding on high
She'll roam where she wants
Come and we'll fly!

THE PINE

Tall proud pine, pencil slim
Laden with cones on each haughty limb.

Needles falling as the breeze calls them down
Covering the grass in a carpet of brown.

NEW BEGINNINGS

Goodnight Moon,
Hello Sun.
A bright new day has just begun.

New beginnings
Exciting they are
Challenged again
I reach for a star.

In a dream I clearly see.
A vision forever
Don't take it from me.

I'll place it before me
Each day that I live
And pray for the happiness
Fulfillment will give.

THOUGHTS

Walking along the beach the wind in my face, how difficult it is to walk into it. I am slow! Then I am reminded that we all walk at our own pace, however we persevere, or what detours we make along the way. We lean into the wind. God says, "Lean on me."

Old Age

MEMORIES

Memories are precious
Stored gently in time.
They thread through our lives
Like cobwebs so fine.

Where would we be
If we couldn't recall...
Moments so tender
Loving acts great and small?

Not only happy times
Tucked far away
Memories hold sadness
We still feel today.

Our life has been shaped
From these hours in time
Our characters formed
Our faces to shine.

And so all these thoughts
My heart will lift
Thank you Oh God!
For this beautiful gift.

OLD AGE... The place we have reached

I agree my friend, old age is not the place
That we would choose to be.
Though in the valley we may dwell
The mountaintops are ours to see.

Those great heights, which we have scaled,
Now beyond our reach.
Do not banish them from view
There is much they can teach.

The valleys can be filled
With happiness and song
We set our face to the life
For which we now belong.

Perhaps it is new friends
Who will brighten up our day.
It is never too late
Again to learn to play.

The game of life, now more sedate
Becomes a challenge new
The dice of life we roll
Despair we will eschew!

Do not give up on humankind
With her do not despair
There are many folk who do work hard
To make our world more fair.

Give thanks for little things
That come to us each day.
Learn to be in the moment
Don't worry what folk say.

You have not lost control
Your skates you will not need
Your way may seem a little rough
So scatter lots of seed.

Seeds of love to help forgive
The worries that you feel.
The pearly gates are there for you
You need a faith that's real!

Focus on the beauty,
The wonders of a child unfold
Like a flower spreads its petals.
We do not need to mould.

Remember
Two men looked through prison bars
One saw mud,
The other stars.

My friend I wish you
Many birthdays still to come
May your days be filled
With many stars and lots of happy fun.

We can't go back to experience the past, so let's look forward to the things that will last. Happiness and love can always be there, if we allow ourselves a full life to share.

THAT MISCHIEVOUS IMP

That mischievous imp
He's stealing my sleep
He tickles and teases
He makes me count sheep.

He seems to delight
In my toss and my turn
He knows that for sleep
I really do yearn.

It seems that he taps
My eyes at his will
They will not close
I lie very still.

Why is he so cruel
This little sprite?
What have I done
To make him fight?

He won't let me go
I get up and walk
He acts quite dumb
Refuses to talk.

I know one day
His power I'll break
It is a matter of will
How long will it take?

I'll try to be wise
And do as I'm told
Do you think
It's about growing old?

If so I long
For the days of my youth,
I'm tired of being
Long in the tooth!

I recall the times
When sleep, was a breeze
Asleep on the pillow
Before you could sneeze.

To sleep a night through,
An unheard of pleasure,
To think a simple act
Was mine to treasure.

Kind folk have told me
Of many a trick,
I pray, and I breathe
Hoping this imp to kick.

One day I know
Just deserts he will get
I'll hang in for now
Wishing we'd never met.

Some wisdom for you,
If he taps on your door
Don't bid him come in
Give him the "what for."

'Cos he's in the business
Of making life hard,
Give him an inch
And he'll take a yard!

Take my advice
Tell him "get lost!"
If not, forever
You'll count the cost!

THAT TROUBLESOME IMP

He's at it again
That troublesome imp
Now he's stolen my breath
He's making me limp!

What more does he want
He's taken my sleep
Now he's looking at more,
He's in deep, very deep.

To work at stealing my breath
My life giving source.
Why would he dare
And why use such force?

Does he not know
The distress that is mine?
Has he no heart?
I guess he feels fine.

Breathing is natural
It's achieved without thought
We take it for granted
Of course as we ought!
He flits through the day,
And prowls in the night
He sits on my chest
And squeezes it tight.

He wakes me and laughs
When I struggle to sit.
To him it's a joke
He enjoys every bit.

I wonder why he's
Picking on me
I hope soon he'll tire
And set me free.

When he uses his magic
It's black and it's cruel.
It leaves you weak
He thinks I'm a fool.

I can see what he's up to!
I'll see this through.
He won't best me
One day he will rue!

I have a weapon
He cannot resist.
A little word called hope
It is something he's missed!

I know he thinks
He'll wear me down
He hates to see me cheerful
It just makes him frown!

The memory I still have
From somewhere long past
Is "hope springs eternal"
Something that will last!

I have a long list of things
Which help to bring hope
That imp cannot compete
He can sit, and just mope.

He needs to hear the story of
The linnet in the park
Who sings before the dawn,
Knowing light will end the dark.

There are many weapons
That I have, he will never rattle.
Give up now you bothersome imp
You'll never win this battle.

A FOREIGN LAND

Where has my body gone?
It is a foreign land.
One day it disappeared
No fanfare, no band!

Had it been spirited away
By someone of ill repute?
Where does a body go,
Who else would it suit?

Perhaps it felt
A new home it would find.
My soul I searched,
Had I been unkind?

After all I had tried
My very best
Had given it a diet
Of health and lovely rest.

Instead I have a body
I really do not know
Unfamiliar now it is
I often feel its woe!

It no longer does my bid
And often does not work
Each day I sit and wonder
What around each hour may lurk.

It could be unfamiliar
Some thing I cannot greet
Any changes now I have to learn
Each difficulty to meet.

Many days I yearn,
To find my body lost,
Did I not realise
How precious was the cost.

Can I redeem the body
I once had,
Can I rescue from the ashes
All that, that makes me sad?

Can I learn to compensate
For what has gone away
Will I receive new grace
To all my fears allay!

If you are outside
Looking in you may not be aware.
You may think my body
Has not gone anywhere!

However it has vanished,
And left me all alone
To struggle with its strangeness
Which is nothing like my own.

I want to feel the welcome
Of the body I once wore,
Everything has changed
Down to its very core!

For what I took for granted
I guess it is farewell.
A new way now of coping
Will my worries quell?

The lesson of this ditty
Is appreciate each day.
Love your body and be kind
No matter what folk say.

Then your body may be spared,
From reaching foreign shore
Cherish it with love
The reward will be much more!

GROWING OLD

We are growing old
What does it really mean?
Will we lose our reason,
What difference will be seen?

Perhaps agility we'll lack
Our bones will ache and rattle
Muscles groaning with each move
Hardship we will battle.

Our gait will slow, we'll walk with care.
A fall may just be risky
To end up with a broken hip
We'd be no longer frisky!

Will we become invisible
As many oldies seem to be?
Cos' younger ones dismiss us
As if they cannot see!

Perhaps it will be the opposite
And we will know esteem
Perhaps we'll be respected
When they realize where we've been.

For oldies have a tale to tell
Which sometimes folk forget,
For each it will be special
We have not finished yet.

There's still a fire burning
We want the world to know
Do not write us off
There is much 'get up and go.'

Inside there beats a heart
The word 'old' does not know
Wait till you get there
You will find that this is so.

Every now and then
We may have a rage.
It is not just the young
Who seem to fit that page.

These words you might ponder
Wonder at will
Please don't forget
There's life in us still!

THAT FOX WANTS TO STEAL MY BOX

A gift box of memories
Although out of sight,
Awaiting their opening.
Will be my delight.
When I'm older with sweet recall
I'll open my box, be held in its thrall.

Every now and then
A thought comes to me.
There is a fox
Who wanders free.
Will that fox take my box?

I hope you have not met him,
Sometimes he pokes his head
Where he should not be.
He delights in scaring you and me.

His name is more than one,
He can appear in any place,
At times I feel to pull his tail
And make him about face.

I guard my box of memories
They are precious and so real
I do not want to lose them
Or give him the chance to steal!

They have been gathered
Sometimes at real cost,
Even those that make me sad
I would hate to see them lost.

Sometimes that fox slips
Through my door,
I think he teases me!
I panic just a little, until He sets me free.

My box is light and happy,
With a little sadness there.
If he gets his hands in it
Darkness it will share.

For when he comes
The light is banished
Our memories fade away
If I'm really careful
Can he be kept at bay?

I'm sure you know his proper name,
Or one of them at least
When we hear we shudder
Our fox can be a beast.

He steals from us a lifetime
Of friends and family dear
Of happy moments spent
When listening ears we've lent.

We are diligent with doing
Crosswords and the rest,
We pray that with memories
Clear we will be blest.

If that fox comes a knocking
We'll pretend we do not hear
He's out to scare us ....
To make us shed a tear.

If you feel him lurking give him not
The time of day
We'll banish him forever
He'll never hold us in his sway!!

YESTERDAY!

Today the child of yesterday
Talked with my grown up self
A conversation we did have
It came from life's high shelf.

We all have things with which
We do not deal
We shelve them and hope,
Perhaps they are not real!

For if there is not reality,
We can pretend they are not there
Deep down we fool ourselves
We do not wish our soul to bare.

Sadly they do not vanish
They are there for all our life
Better now to dust them
Before they cause us strife.

They will hassle us forever
Insidiously they will niggle
Do not entertain them
Or like a worm they'll wriggle!

You may find they make us ill
As they settle in our mind
Like a ghost haunting us
These thoughts can be unkind.

They will chastise and berate
Guilt will be our trip
Don't put them again on our shelf
They're sure to hold their grip.

Instead bring them down
Forgiveness may be the key
Our self or others
Whoever it may be.

They have already resided there
For far too long
Do away with them
It's time to join life's song.

See them for what they are
A reminder of the past
Things change from day to day
Our values now will last.

We cannot be defined
By mishaps from long ago.
While we carry them
Our souls may just not grow.

Once again we'll celebrate
At last we've glimpsed the light.
Now our shelf is dusted
Our hearts are happy and bright.

Lord...
Help us to remember that there is no dividing line between the spiritual and the secular...
That all we do should be an expression of your life and love.
Lift our hearts that all may be to your glory.

THE CARNIVAL IS OVER

Life is but a merry-go-round
The fun of the fair
The noise of the band.

Shouting and laughter
And hearts that are light
We dance and play
For most of the night.

Another day dawns
The carnival still.
No longer do crowds the
Fairground fill.

Gone are the clowns
Balloons and the floss
The trash in the gutter
The silent dross.

It's hard to believe
We were once a part.
So little remains to
Warm our heart.

Cool breeze of the evening
Steals across the sky.
We're all alone
Life's gone with a sigh.

A broken string---interrupted melody....romance has died.

Talking to God

TRAPPED

I'm caught in a web
Of intricate mesh
Each way that I move
Just hurts me afresh.

I helped to weave
This prison of mine
A captive I am
In gossamer fine.

Can you untangle
These strands for me?
Please from this web
Will you set me free?

THOUGHT

I saw my garden bare
I felt the poverty of Spirit
Where are you, Lord?

BEND TO MY WILL

Did I hear you right Lord?
I prayed that you might heal
And in my spirit heard you say
Embrace my child,
Embrace just how you feel.

How can I do this Lord?
Will you not give me a sign?
Your word tells me to pray
That healing will be mine

Is there a missing link
Something I do not know
Is there a formula to follow,
Am I yet to grow?

I have read the book
It's not as easy as I thought
The do's and don'ts of healing
Have I not done as I ought?

I have heard from many sources
Miracles of love and grace.
Why are my prayers not heard
Have you from me turned your face?

Forgive me Lord for doubting you
Help me to clearly see
You have not moved from me
Instead you've set me free!

How could I forget that in
Your word I read
Upon your palm I'm written.
And like a shepherd you will lead.

I know that you will walk with me.
I will never be alone.
Your healing power of love and grace
The hope that you have sown.

Content I now will be
And try to understand
Your ways are not our ways
You have our future planned.

I will rejoice and give thanks
That you my spirit fill.
In gratitude I will embrace
And bend now to your will.

NEW YEAR'S DAY

I wonder what God has planned for me to do in this New Year?
I pray for new dimensions in faith, an excited expectancy
Today a new beginning on the threshold I stand
Before me a year of promise.
Lord help me to wait on you,
To be still and know that you are God.
Grant me a patient heart to see your will and purpose for my life
That I may serve you obediently and effectively
To your name be honour and glory. Amen.

TEARS IN A BOTTLE

Your word, Oh Lord is full of your love! A canvas blank on which is splashed wonderful imagery of your great concern for us.

Right now I'm thinking of that lovely psalm which tells us that You collect our tears in a bottle. The God of all the universe who cares for us so much, that this illustration can be used!!

I love it! Think of all the tears that are shed over a lifetime....And some day perhaps in Heaven we will find a bottle with our name on. Full of those very same tears!

It is such a comforting thought, even though we know that the imagery is to show us the wonderful love which God has for us, imagery is such a powerful tool to help our understanding.

The psalmist has used this illustration actually taken from a custom in the time in which he lived. In those days it was customary that when a man went off to fight he gave his wife or sweetheart a bottle in which she would collect the tears of sadness because she was missing him. When he returned she would present him with the bottle and he would see her sadness and her love for him.

In this Psalm it is God who collects tears... The times of loss, of grief, ill health, all the times when for one reason or another we have experienced sadness, He is saying to us, "you really matter to me. I love you with an everlasting love.... I am with you in your times of sadness. I care so much I collect your tears in my bottle!"

This tells me that the God of the Universe loves you and me more than we can ever imagine.... That he is with us in all life's ups and downs. When next we shed tears, perhaps we may recall this lovely picture and know that we are not alone. Our God is walking with us. He is collecting our tears in his bottle.

THE WORLD OF SYMBOLS

Thank you Lord for the world of symbols
The commonplace
A loaf of bread...reminding me that you have said
That you are the bread of life.
Our nourishment, all that we need.

A candle shedding its light into the darkest corner
Giving us the assurance of your words....
That you are the light of the world.
That great light that shines to lead us and guide us.

The same light that shines into the darkest corners of our lives.
Bringing the opportunity to seek forgiveness.
I could go on and on.

We thank you Lord for speaking to us in our everyday life
through our ordinary experience.
Symbols are powerful.

DARKNESS TO LIGHT

Lord
Your timing is so right.
Thank you for the darkness
You turn again to light.

Bitter painful hurts,
Hidden down so deep
You help us each to bear them
And share with us our grief.

Your faithfulness and love
Surrounds us still
Until our barren spirit
Cried out for you to fill.

Perhaps we have not felt
Your presence in our pain,
But you were there with arms outstretched.
You called us by our name.

So thank you Lord, you walk with us,
In happiness and pain
Giving us new hope
To live our lives again.

Looking to the brightest star
God help us to find
The wholeness you created us for.

SAVING GRACE

My mind's a blank
I feel at loss
How do I get my point across?
I only hope that as I grope
For words to fill the space
That they will come so easily
And be my saving grace!

ROLE PLAY

You understand Lord
The roles we often play
Perhaps we are unaware of
Whom we've been today
Is it that we play a part,
The script we read
Not really from our heart?

So perhaps this is a
Plea and prayer for grace
For others to see and face
The fact that sometimes
We are not the folk we seem to be
But would love to be ourselves and free.

So Lord we thank you for being there to care
When feelings of frustrations come
We can come to you to share.
You see beyond our actions
To the motives in our heart.
You know then sometimes why
We need to play a part!

MASKS

Do you wear a mask?
I know I often do
Sometimes it just happens
Those times I often rue.

It is like having a selection
Hanging on the wall
In passing I decide
Will it be one or all!

We know it doesn't happen
Quite like that
It seems to be innate that peg
On which we hang our hat.

It seems that often
There is for us a need
To be present to the other
In a way that they can read.

I have heard myself described
To my disbelief
I know that it is not me.
Much to my relief!

The experience with that person
Has meant I've donned a mask
Perhaps it was necessary
There was no need to ask!

When we look at life
In all its complex wonder
We see the ways we interact
Is often without number.

Today I am tentative
Perhaps I am unsure.
You would look at me
And think there is not more.

Tomorrow I could be confident
Even a little bold
The situation and the folk
Help the stance I hold.

If that is so, do not despair
Do not even doubt
Perhaps being all things to all people
Is what we are about!

WANDERING THOUGHTS

If you are given a vision in life
Don't relinquish your grip
Just hold on tight.
Do not be discouraged
By those who dismiss the magic of dreams
Bringing searched for bliss.

A PRAYER

Take the broken fragments of my life
I offer them to you...
The Master Potter whose gentle hand
Will lovingly renew.

Take my offering small and mould me to your will
Lord help me to be humble
My empty heart
Your Spirit fill.

WE'LL PLANT A SEED

We'll plant a seed together
And water it each day.
A seed of love to carry
Each task that comes our way.

This gift we'll nurture carefully
As with each other we will share.
We'll nurture it with joy
To show how much we care.

If we do not plant,
But instead that precious seed we keep,
Our lives will surely miss
The harvest we can reap.

It is in giving we receive,
Tho' sometimes hard to face.
Don't puzzle over this,
Just accept this happy grace.

So let us gather.
We'll sing a joyful tune.
That slender stem will grow
And bring its special bloom.

I will no longer ponder on what's ahead to see
But accept in all humility the plan worked out for me.

TALKING TO GOD!

Lord
Right now I'm feeling sorry for myself
Really sorry,
In fact that real door mat feeling.

Do you know what I mean?
That feeling that everyone is
Walking over me!
Children wrapped up in
Countless activities.

Husband committed to work involvement
I seem to be ready to jump at their beck and call.
I'm tired of being taken for granted
Forgive me for indulging in self-pity.

I guess it is part of our experience in life
I feel at times I want to run, put distance between us
So that I can be a person again,
Lord you gave us self worth.

Help them to see that I need this assurance
this affirmation.

Help us to live together. So that the scales may not
Be tipped one way or another.
That there might be a happy balance
In all our relationships.
Amen.

I searched and I searched,
Lord only to find...you were there all the time.

GRATITUDE!

A thing of beauty is a
Grateful heart,
If you have one
You're blessed to be part!

Part of a family
Who has learnt how to be
Thankful in all things
Most folk would agree!

We all know someone
Who fits this bill!
Whether big or small
These shoes they would fill.

Sometimes we're discouraged
When we see our selfish greed.
Especially when our eyes are opened
To see our brother's need!

If we can just say thank you
In a very simple way
It is a habit that will become
Part of every day!

A thankful heart gives rise to wonder
We can catch it from each other
It will put a smile upon our face,
As we talk with one another.

If we are grateful for each day
And what the hours bring
A happy feeling will be ours
With joy our spirit's sing.

If we do not have this
Special gift, It is an attitude
Learnt behaviour it can be
We can all have gratitude!

MY CUP OF BLESSINGS

Come share my cup of blessings
It is waiting here for you
Full to overflowing
It will our lives renew.

Blessings given freely
Are meant to give away
Don't jealously hide them
They are here for us today.

Some hug them to their chest
Or in their fist so tight
Come spread the joy they bring
It will make you happy and bright.

Blessings are little miracles
That sometimes we do not see,
We take for granted all we're given
I know you will agree.

So bring your cup to help me
To share this wondrous gift
We'll give our blessings freely.
It will our spirits lift.

A MORNING PRAYER

The symphony of morning
My heart sang...
Praise, praise your Holy Name.

Today I was asked what were some amazing experiences I could recall drawn from the course of my life. I began to think back.

AMAZING

Amazing! Isn't all life full of amazement?
Isn't it wonderful, happy, sad and all the in between?
Bittersweet, satisfaction, sorrow and loss
What a gamut of emotions are let loose
In this beautiful gift we have been given.

This fragile gift we hold in our hands carefully
So precious it is, how vulnerable we are
It is ours to use as we please.
That is why it is a gift, a gesture of grace
It is ours to choose how we will live it.

We can keep our fists closed tight and
Keep this gift to ourselves guarding it carefully.
Or we can gloriously open our hands
And hearts and let it fly free.
And then the rewards will follow.

Rewards that no one can put a value on!
It cannot be estimated. Our life cup will overflow
It takes so little to help another to smile
To be a listening ear, or a comfort
To a friend in distress!

Our amazing life - Full of wonder
Dreams that sometimes come true
Others as yet not realised, perhaps may never be.
We do not give up even when things
Are not as we imagined they should be.

Be thankful for this life we have been given
There is magic in gratitude, it softens hearts
It warms our spirits, it encourages us
In hope and hope is a
Vital ingredient in this amazing adventure.

Yes! Life is an adventure
Whether we have mountains to climb
Or valleys to cross. I suspect
We will have both, Sometimes we will
Be up sometimes down!

But we will never lose our
Sense of amazing wonder at
That which has been given to us.
Life in all its fullness, happy or sad.
Our cup runs over!

So to my friend who poses this question, I have no singular answer.
My life cup has been full of blessings!

WHERE ARE YOU LORD?

Where are you Lord?
At present you seem so far away.
Many of us are in isolation
Our hearts and minds are trapped,
On every side we are flooded with
Images of illness and death.

Have you left us Lord?
Are you unhappy with us
Your children?

Why are you silent?
We need your help as never before
Your people are weeping,
We cannot see our way
Our focus is fixed on
Keeping our distance from each other.

Have you left us Lord?
Are you unhappy with us
Your children?

This virus has appeared
It seems right out of the blue.
Unbidden its cruel arms reaching
Out to crush us mere mortals.
We shake our heads
Can you feel our despair?

Have you left us Lord?
Are you unhappy with us
Your children?

Some of us we are told
Are more vulnerable than others,
Those whose health is already compromised
Those who are frail and aged
Children afraid for their parents
Who fall into this category.

Have you left us Lord?
Are you unhappy with us
Your children?

Your people are sad,
Their tears are freely flowing
Many have lost their livelihoods
They have families to support
Which way will they turn
They face a brick wall.

Have you left us Lord?
Are you unhappy with us
Your children?

And yet outside my window
The sun is still shining,
It is bright and happy,
The trees are green
And the birds are still singing
Your lovely gift of creation.

And so you are reassuring me
Dear Lord that you have not given
Up on us your children.
Your gifts are still with us
And your healing is there.
For each of us.

Help us to rise above our circumstance,
To reach out to you knowing that
Your promises have stood for your people
In the past and they stand unchanged today.
Your love for us is firm and sure.
Forgive us for doubting you.

We know that you look at our world and
Feel the sadness of each one of us
You are our Father and your heart weeps
For your bleeding creation
You are one with us as we face
This hardship together.

Why? Is the question that may be on our lips,
The answer we will never know
However my Lord our trust is in you
Another to place in our Mystery box.
We will continue to pray with thanksgiving
For what we have been given.

We will pray for our Governments,
Our leaders who have to make hard decisions for us,
We will pray for each other that we might
Be an encouragement as we navigate these uncharted waters
Above all we will pray for our hurting world that
We may be healed.

Amen

Weary I am in body and soul
Renewal I seek to make me whole.

CHURCH FESTIVALS

THE CHRISTMAS TREE

Each year the Christmas tree
Is dragged from its hiding place
A suitable spot is chosen
And there the room does grace.

Then out comes my memory bag
The part I really love
It's full of lots of baubles
And the Angel for above!

There are elves in red and green
Bells of silver and tinsel of gold
Baby Jesus, Joseph and Mary
Their story is retold.

To see it standing there
A touch of magic is for me
Its sparkling lights are twinkling
On our happy Christmas tree.

THE WISE MAN

I am one of the three wise men
Some called us the Magi from the east.
We visited and gifted the new born baby
Little did we know here lay the King of Kings.

Today, many have not heard our great story,
Have not shared in the wonder of this miracle of birth,
It has been consigned to the basket of folklore
Even for those whom have heard, it is not real.
They have not known the wonder of that special time.

God called the three of us from a far away country,
We followed that lustrous star which went before
Leading and guiding us to that Royal place!
To many it was a simple stable to us it was so much more.

We came bearing gifts, gifts for a king,
Gold, myrrh and frankincense!
To lay at his feet,
In this simple place we felt a sense of awe.
We worshipped him! Somehow knowing
This was not a mere babe!

The years have passed, we have grown old.
I am now the only Magi left,
I sit and reflect. Reflect on the happenings on that night long ago.
I have seen and heard much, heard stories
Telling of this baby growing into manhood
Heard wonderful tales of goodness, of miracles!

His wonderful message of love which he spoke into
Our suffering world. A message which would
Reverberate through the ages, bringing comfort over and over again
And then the cruelty and shame of the crucifixion.
This was the end!

But wait! This could not be. God had spoken to us long ago.
In the Heavens the Angels had been rejoicing when
He gave us his Son.
This was never the end.... Instead it was the beginning....
Even I, a humble Magi who had been honoured by the call of God
To worship all those years ago, could sense in my Spirit that this
was
A momentous happening.
The world would never be the same.
God raised Him to life.
He gave us His precious life giving Spirit,
Before going home to live with His Father!

What an honour I have been given....
Called to worship the King of all Glory,
If only I could look down the years,
And see the impact this will have on humankind
What will happen to his followers?
Already they are facing persecution!
To stand for a faith,
With such a beginning will not be easy.
It is a faith that was born in the
Simplicity of Love.
Not a movement that will grow from the charismatic leadership
Of a great conqueror, but the son of a carpenter!
I wonder!!

GOOD FRIDAY PEOPLE

We are Good Friday people
This we truly know
We suffer we are flawed
Our spirit tells us so.

In a way we are called to
Walk the way of the Cross
We are vulnerable, weak
Jesus takes away the dross.

My musings often take me
To that scene so long ago
When the babe of Bethlehem
Was born in stable low.

His message one of love
His time on earth was brief
His followers, his family
Suffered so much grief.

Simon stepped forward
To shoulder the cross
His eyes filled with tears
He began to feel loss.

Peter His beloved disciple
Three times cast him aside
His fear was so great
He from Him did hide.

His supporters were many
We are not told their names
They loved their Master
With no claim to fame.

Of these nameless ones I think
And wonder at their story
For together we have shared
The Lord of all glory.

No one really understood
What happened on that day
Now centuries on
Folk find the shades of grey.

However like those of old
Many have heard his call
The Easter story has touched our hearts
Has held us in its thrall.

It has burst as a golden ball
Of light flooding our soul
With the hope of the Holy one,
Jesus makes us whole.

He is our rescuer
He is our friend.
Our troubled lives
He is ready to mend.

Good Friday people we may be
There is a shining ray
Let us not forget
The joy of Easter Day!

So accept the many blessings
That we find along our way
His victory o'er the cross
Has won for you this day.

THE SPIRIT

I really wonder why I cannot be
Like the Saints of old
When your Spirit set them free?

On that day we saw that
Peter preached with zeal.
He left behind forever his fears that were so real.

For your spirit had emboldened him
With courage true and rare
It was with great conviction he spoke your name
To all who gathered there.

And yet my Lord I know
That same power you offer me
Why do I fail to trust and great Your servant be?

So take my life, my faltering steps I give to you
Create in me a wholeness,
Your loving spirit forever renew.

THOUGHTS

Deep within me an imprisoned spirit lies
It longs for self-expression
How oft I hear its cries.
Sometimes so eloquent, whilst others frustration bound,
Almost incoherent... where can the key be found?

PENTACOST

In the rush of the mighty wind
The gentle touch of the breeze
Spirit of God you come to me
From a life of Bondage to set me free.

The flame of your fire consumes me
My heart is filled with your love
Showers of blessing fall gently around
Peace steals upon me, with joy I abound.

Fill me forever...my spirit cries out
I pray I'll not grieve you, please gird me about
Kindle the flame of love in my heart
Help me with others this Gift to impart.

CHRISTMAS EVE

Christmas Eve, long, long ago,
A gracious old home
I remember it so.

Wide bay windows framed the room.
Logs by the hearth
Would be blazing soon.

Tucked in the corner a green pine stood
Together we'd decorated
It looked so good.

Glitter and tinsel and Christmas red
The white shining angel
Far above our head.

No doorway was missed as holly we hung
With the sounds of our laughter
The old house rung.

Up in the nursery baby slept
Far in the heavens
Stars their watch kept.

The crisp night air began to ring
With the music and joy
That carollers bring.

A light blanket of snow began to fall
We gazed in delight
A fairyland to enthral.

Warm and snug in the spirit of love
We climbed to our beds
On the floor up above.

Sleep overcomes us as drowsy we lay
Happiness comes
On Christmas day!

CHRISTMAS 2013

Christmas is.....
A candle burning bright
It sheds its light upon us.
And offers us new sight.

As family we gather
To celebrate God's sign
We'll share His love together
And drink His Kingdom wine.

A sign of peace and hope
Each year He gives anew
That ancient star still shining
Her brilliance breaking through.

Year after year we listen
As the story is retold.
We come the Christ child to adore
As did the wise of old.

THE LONE SHEPHERD

Out on the hillside
Beyond the city wall
The lone shepherd
Once again heard the call.

He was now an old man
His ears becoming deaf,
A call from within
So clear, he caught his breath.

He knew that voice
For the last three years
It had lovingly calmed
His many fears!

It all seemed so long ago
That wonderful night
When the Angel appeared
The hillside bathed in light.

He heard again the words that rang
"Fear not, tidings of great joy "
Praise the birth
Of this little boy!

Over all this time
He had hoped to hear more
Steeped in obscurity
The boy obeyed God's law.

Now the babe of Bethlehem
The Son of God they say
Being mocked and jeered
Hateful was the fray!

The years had gone
Long ago he had lost his youth
He knew this young man.
Spoke the truth.

He had thought much
On that one time event
Waiting,
And then he found what was meant!

The crowd had gathered
On the shore.
Jesus spoke to their needs
But there was so much more.

That day he felt his heart burning
He knew that this was his God
Ready now to follow
He would walk the way Jesus had trod.

The shepherd looked with sadness
The Easter story unfold
He was but a simple man
But knew this had been foretold.

A stable...it was simple and bare. And there you lay
...The King of all the earth.

THE CHRISTMAS CANDLE

Light the candle Oh! My Love
We'll clap our hands in joy.
The flames will flicker in delight
We'll welcome one small boy.

Light the candle Oh! My Love
There's awe and wonder here.
The Angels sing on high
The Shepherds quake in fear.

Light the candle Oh! My Love
Its light we'll shed abroad
The whole wide world will know
We have received our Lord.

Light the candle Oh! My Love
For all who hurt this night
For when the morning dawns
Their burden will be light.

Light the candle Oh! My Love
Let the flames burn warm and strong.
We have a melody to sing
Come join us in our song.

Light the candle Oh! My Love
It will help us find our way.
The slender cord that binds
Will hold us in its sway.

The candle has been lit My Love
All is clear and bright.
We'll usher in this Christmas morn
And greet the coming light.

PENTECOST SUNDAY

Today is Pentecost Sunday, so Happy Birthday to the church! Below is a little poem that I wrote at Pentecost a few years ago. Thought! The Holy Spirit is depicted as wind at times in the Old Testament and as we celebrate today we read that in the New Testament the Spirit came to the disciples on the day of Pentecost as the rush of a mighty wind. We read the story of Elijah in the Old Testament who experienced the still small voice of the Spirit. Often God speaks to us this way heart to heart.

The thought here is of God being playful, delighting in His child. I like this imagery as sometimes we forget the great pleasure that He feels when He sees us.

There are times when we do feel that we stand on Holy ground (with Angels all around).
Xxxx.
Kay

THE WIND OF THE SPIRIT

The evening hours had stilled a storm
The wind came whispering in the early morn,
Whilst flowers their petals scattered at ease.
It tapped on my window I heard it say
"awaken my child, it's time to play."
It stole through my door with barely a sigh,
And danced on my desk setting papers a-fly.

It laughed as it played with the strands of my hair
I breathed in with pleasure the cool sweet air
It tickled the mantle that had me cast down,
With gladness I stepped from the weight of its frown.

Tis' the wind of the Spirit, a still small voice,
A heart to heart whisper in which I rejoice.
Sometimes you speak in the roar of the sea,
Today Lord you came in the gentle breeze.

I think of Elijah, the prophet of old
His troubles were great, his faith was bold.
When backed in a corner with fears beset,
You spoke on the wind and his needs you met.

In this early hour on holy ground I stand
Your peace is gently flowing across this great Southland.
Smiling at my window now are rays of morning sun.
My joyful heart is grateful
Come Spirit come!

EASTER MORNING AT NOOSA

No my Lord
Not the palms and olives
To greet my eyes this day,
But the gentle casuarinas
Dancing in full sway.

The greetings of the lorikeets
Their hallelujahs ring.
Creation gives you glory,
As through the earth it sings.

Out on the spit, the seagulls
Garbed in robes of white
A choir of the morning
To say farewell to night.

Grey clouds now are banished
With the breaking of the dawn
Golden sunshine ushers in
Your resurrection morn.
Amen.

14. Noosa's beautiful beach.

CHRISTMAS 1980

You came to man so humbly
Your glory laid aside
In stable bare and simple
You came to turn the tide.

To show to us so clearly
The love of Father God
He knew we'd only find it
By tracing the steps you trod.

And so Oh! Lord this Christmas
My thoughts are filled with you
The wonder of the Christ child
Just fills my heart anew.

And though I'll always love
The things we all hold dear
Keeping customs old
That come but once a year.

But through it all
My prayer will be —
The festive time will bring
A sense of joy and wonder,
As we praise our Lord and King.

This Christmas as we celebrate...let our birthday gift to you
Be a grateful heart.

Social Justice

PRAYER FOR JUSTICE

They're hungry Lord
And I feel satisfied
The pangs I feel
They do not hurt.

I'm complacent
I don't want to be.
I cry out for justice
I want my involvement to be real.

But somewhere along the way
The enthusiasm wanes
Deep sorrow
But where is the spirit of yesterday
That burning zeal!

I want to help Lord
Please fan the flame
Don't let the fire go out.

Over the years my brother Russell and I have corresponded by sharing verse. At times I have responded in like manner. He wrote the little poem below when reflecting on the turn over of our Prime Ministers. As you will see read acrostically, he suggests Peppa Pig would fit the bill.
(a well-loved character known to most of our young children)

The poem **PEPPA PIG** is my response to him.............a bit of fun!"

POEM TO KAY FROM BROTHER RUSSELL

Prime Ministers aren't permanent, or that's how they just seem,
Every second year or so, they're punted by their team,
Polls - they are the problem, at least that's what they say,
Press and Media, they all helped, to bring on that fateful day,
A Pollster knocked upon my door, he asked how I would vote,
Perhaps for Bill or Tone or Mal, but was shocked with what I wrote,
I don't want those, I said with scorn - them I wouldn't feed,
Go read this poem acrostically, you'll see who's best to lead.

PEPPA PIG

Who is Miss Peppa Pig?
To read of her prowess
I guess she's someone big!
Not in size mind you,
So fame must be her gig!

Indeed I am intrigued
She truly must be rare
Do you think her pedigree
She'll really want to bare?

Are you sure the next P.M.
She will be?
Will her snout be in the trough
Will she diddle you and me?

When the pollster
Knocks upon your door
Will you speak of Peppa
Will you say she's honest to the core?

The only problem I can see
Is that Peppa is a pig
Will she try to save her bacon
Or perhaps not care a fig.

Will she take care of refugees,
Will she put her people first?
Will she be just and fair,
Address the plight of all who thirst?

We are weary of those
Who would self-interest seek.
They do not want to listen
They have their own agenda deep!

So perhaps Peppa Pig
Is the way that we should go.
We'll give her our vote.
The others we will give
The old heave ho!

So full steam ahead,
In your wisdom I will soak.
The only problem is we do not want.
"A pig in a poke!"

PRAYER FOR REFUGEES

This morning I pray for the refugee.
The lonely and the lost
Their life has lost its meaning
They've learnt to count the cost.

Their days are filled with emptiness
A future sad and bleak
Why can't we show compassion?
Give them the home they seek.

Have we walked a mile with them?
Have we with their shoes been shod?
It seems to me to be the way
That we've been shown by God.

The world is just a village
In which we play a part
Can we turn our face away,
And harden yet our heart.

Can it be true you do not hear
The crying in the night?
Do not turn away,
From those in dire plight!

Open your arms and heart
Do not let it stony be,
All the lost really want,
Is to have a home, be free.

Do not close them in,
In prisons like you do
Please see their desperation
Deep down they're just like you!

Please take the time
In this great gift of life,
To ask ourselves, how we can help
To ease our brother's strife?

For family we are all
We may have a different skin,
We may speak another language
We're all the same within.

The mandate God has given
Holds now and for all time
Love each other ...He has said.
'Twas part of his design.

I'm sure when He created
Each one to be His child,
His plan was for a world
That we would not defile.

So let us practise kindness
Compassion and the rest.
Hold up in prayer today
Those who find their life a test.

That they may be refreshed
And see this trial through
That families are reunited
May be filled with hope anew.

Pray for them and for
The powers that be
That hearts may melt,
With Mercy running free.

WE HAVE A PROBLEM

Our world has a problem
Or is it an opportunity?
Can we help our fellow man
To live free as a community?

The word Refugee is to some
As red rag to a bull
They cannot see the human side
They want their coffers full.

The Internet is feeding us
With lots of hateful stuff
Some is quite offensive,
People are so rough.

I'm tired of reading ditties
With language quite obscene
Folk who think they speak for all
Do they think we're green?

A special kind of hate incited
They may not think it so
The excuse they give they're
Helping keep the status quo!

Where does their info come
Why are they downright rude!
There can be no excuse
I just think they're crude!

There is gross exaggeration,
In what they have to say
They infer they speak for all of us
Don't give them time of day!

Their irreverence is total
No tolerance for others.
There's no love or respect
For our hurting brothers.

How many Muslims do you know,
As persons I would ask?
Are they demanding Sharia?
No! So take yourselves to task.

Are you familiar with the Gospel,
Do you know what Jesus said?
He asks us to love each other
Is it something you've not read?

He asked us to love our enemies.
It is really a command
We cannot pick and choose
Love and peace walk hand in hand.

If we are Christians
Look to the Sermon on the Mount
There we will find the mind of Christ,
Water from a living fount.

So will you think before you
Pen another line
Compassion from your heart
Now would be the time.

Do not stir up trouble
Surely our goal is peace.
We should be in the solution
That will see our problems cease.

So if an email comes your way
In the style of the above,
Do not choose to pass it on,
It will be your act of love.

THE HOMELESS

Lord....
I see him in the shopping centre
Each time I go to buy
He always looks the same.
I sometimes want to cry.

His clothes are tattered,
His feet are bare
Is there anyone to really care?

Perhaps he does not have a home
A place to lay his head
Where does he sleep,
Is he properly fed?

Sometimes he's searching in the bin
My heart cries out to think of him.
Sometimes we want to feel you near
Yet fail to see your presence in your child so dear.

Amen

REFLECTION FROM MEALS ON WHEELS

It is a shabby little house
Standing all alone
The garden quite unloved
And very overgrown.

Inside she sits burdened
By her age
Amidst reminders of her life
Now a forgotten page.

The homeliness that once was there
Replaced with sad neglect
Where are her friends her family
Who once did her respect?

Patiently she sits and waits
With solitary plate and mug.
How I long to hold her,
Give her a caring hug.

Cheerfully she greets us
Hiding how she feels.
If only we could help her more
Than just delivering Meals on Wheels.

An aching void...again alone
How much can one soul bare?
The God of all does not desert...forever He'll be there.

HE DRINKS TOO MUCH

He drinks too much.
What can we do?
He looks for help
But won't carry it through.

He feels self-pity
No one cares
He is a failure
With whom can he share?

His life's a wheel
Going round and round
He won't jump off
Let his feet touch the ground.

That cycle's so safe
No reality's there
To face life as it is
Would be too much to bear.

And so we support
But in the end
The first step is yours
My troubled friend.

Reflections

FEELINGS
Why is there a barrier
When feelings are exposed?
Yes! It takes courage
To bare our inner soul.

But like a flower opening
New life comes blossoming forth.
As we in real communion
Find joy in becoming whole.

SIT AND REFLECT

It sits at gentle anchor, that craft so small and free
I love its fluid lines, its beauty do I see
There's something very peaceful 'bout a boat at mooring still.
It makes me feel so gentle and takes away ill will
So I would say not being too direct,
Perhaps we need to take more time
To sit and just reflect.

I WANT TO BE FREE

I want to be free
I need to walk alone,
Away from the clamour
And din of this world.

I want to find a place,
Of peace that speaks to my heart,
Where I can hear the universe sing
A place where the melody is not lost,
Swallowed in the noise of this life.

I'll walk alone in the trees
Let them speak in their majesty,
Great forests of green
Stretching to the sky
Whispering their secrets in
The gentle breeze.

The flowers in full bloom will
Lift my spirits. My heart will open
I will rejoice. The wild birds
Winging their way in the early morn
Their songs filling the sweet air
Will renew me.

I will walk by the shore
Tasting the tang of ocean spray
I will embrace the wonder of that special place
Feeling at one with the timeless tide
I will find a shell, pressing it close to my ear
It will whisper to me the secrets of life.

Across the dunes I'll wander
I'll greet the Pandanus there,
Across my mind will dance memories
From long ago, I will recall the happy times
The joy of childhood dreams.

It is in quietness that our souls are free
To explore our inner thoughts, to feel at one with nature
To marvel at the beauty that can fill our lives if
We only just open our eyes to behold the wonder.

The wonder of the stream that flows o'er tiny pebbles,
The overhanging willow that caresses the riverbank
Flowers in bud gently opening to greet the day.
Splashes of colour
To store for days of grey.
Are you like me?
Do you also feel the need
To walk free?

NOSTALGIA

Familiar scent of perfume
A long forgotten touch
Nostalgia creeps upon me
The past I loved so much.

Our yesterdays are parcels
We wrap in sheer delight
Unpleasant times we carefully store
In places out of sight.

Forgetting that we cannot dwell
On what has gone before
We lose our vision for today
And fail to reach for more.

WHO WOULD A POET BE?

Who would a poet be?
Would it be you,
Would it be me?

Who will be our source
What will we use?
Perhaps it's inspiration
Innate to every muse.

I wish to make you happy,
With words that will delight
I will call upon my inner child
To help with new insight.

The written word can bring
Emotions to the fore
When it reaches out with love
It will touch our very core.

It can heal the hurting heart,
Sing comfort to the sad,
It will smooth the troubled water
Until our souls are glad.

Words are an art form
A canvas not in sight.
Colour splashed at will
To help our minds take flight.

There is a little poet
In each of us I'm sure.
Let us each reach to the other
To unlock this special door!

USING TIME TO REFLECT

Somehow we seem to need
Those times without the sun.
Perhaps our spirits aren't as light
And our hearts not full of fun
As when the skies are blue
With creation all around,
Sparkling in its golden hue.

But then the sombre mood
Of clouds of heavy grey
Somehow seems to speak to us
In quite another way.

A time to rest--A time to think
Of what, our life can be
A chance for quiet reflection
When many things we see.

So, do not feel discouraged
When days seem dull and grey
Just take time to use them
In a constructive way.

THOUGHTS FOR ANOTHER DAY

Sometimes I feel so lithe and free
My spirit dances joyfully
And so I've learnt to tuck away
Each happy thought for another day.
Then I have found
When stormy times abound
In place of pictures grey
A ray of sunlight lights my way.

WORDS SPOKEN BY THE POET RUMI!

"The world is like a mountain. Your echo depends on you."

What a wonderful piece of prose to reflect on. I know that when I first heard it, it really resonated with me. It made me wonder what my own echo would be.

Would it reverberate strongly? Or would it be weak, one you would strain to hear? Lots of thoughts followed on! How do we find that echo? How do we make it happen? Is it like an imprint on the sand, will it vanish with the incoming tide? How difficult it is to assess our own life experience.

Perhaps the key we need to unlock this mystery is love. When we love we give, and we know that the good Book tells us that when we do this, it comes back ten fold. When we answer with gentle words and put aside our anger, the Echo resounds in like manner! When we are angry and shout, in a similar manner the echo returns to us as it was sent.

The echo can take many forms. Sometimes it comes to us in practical ways. When we have given of ourselves in helping others, we may be surprised in the way it returns to us. Similarly we may give of our material wealth, the echo may come to us in the way that we may never go without.

We can have a sense of excitement about this. We never know how this blessing will return, however we do know that it will.

To be gentle with each other, and be ready to lend a helping hand when it is necessary is a good way to live our lives. Let us hope that we can live in to this mystery and our lives can become a blessing of beautiful echoes!

If we speak to each in tones so rough and harsh, is it any wonder together we cannot laugh?

MY GIFT TO YOU

I cannot draw for you a work of art.
Why I would not know just where to start
Nor could I boldly splash a picture great
With easel and with palette and lots of coloured paint.

However with my pen I'll very humbly try
To strike a chord and help your senses fly,
For with imagination the written word can be
A joy and a delight, a masterpiece to see.

HIGH ABOVE THE CLOUDS

High above the clouds I fly
In a tranquil sea of blue.
Snowy fleeces far below
Create a glorious hue.

I'm here in all the beauty
Of a moment set in time.
I feel it is never ending
Infinity is mine.

SEIZE THE DAY

Softly, sweetly the night is falling,
Not a worry is in sight
Evening warmth enfolding me
The day is tucked in tight.

Some days are easy to walk
Others go so wrong
Why is it difficult our demons to face,
Why can't we all be strong?

In the early morn we wake
A canvas blank we paint
Our brush strokes we will choose
Are we sinner perhaps we're saints?

Fine intentions do we have
Why don't they bear their fruit?
Instead we find that other things
Are crowding to take root.

We have to balance every hour
With whatever comes our way
Learn to live in it with courage
Carpe Diem... Seize the day!

A PRAYER

Lord---
We can't all walk at the same pace
You never expected us to.
So help us not to put distance between each other
But to live together in patience and love.

THE FLEDGLING

I'm glad the fledgling learnt to fly.
Spread her wings and soared on high
Her fears she flung to the passing breeze
As she dipped and dived with graceful ease.

I am that little fledgling
I've learnt to spread my wings.
Now I know the magic
The freedom that it brings!

At times we need a gentle hand
To help us from the nest
It may have been our comfort zone,
A place to sit and rest.

Oh! The joy of finding
Beyond ourselves much more.
We learn to own our feelings
And find our very core.

Along the road there walks
The Lord of all days.
He shares with us our journey
And guides us through life's maze.

We are born to live in the love of God
Lets us claim our birthright.

THE LIGHT IN THE WINDOW

The light in the window
The times of darkness! Friend or foe?
Do you find the hours dragging?
I pray it is not so.

I gaze upon your window
And see your light so bright
Like a beacon shining
To help me pass the night.

Sleep the great eluder
Which clutches me so tight
Hugs me to herself
As a jealous lover might.

She will not let me go
Until new light is born
I rise with heavy heart
Feeling dull and quite forlorn.

Light is a comfort
As a candle flickering low
It shines across our darkness
As it heals and helps us grow.

My silent friend
As I struggle with each hour
To see your light across the way
Somehow gives me power.

Power to defeat those demons
Our enemies of sleep
Determined to annoy us
Their vengeance they will reap.

So together we will fight
They will not have their way
We will show them it is we
Who hold them in our sway.

LITTLE PIECES OF LIGHT

We all need little pieces of light
To help us find our way,
From the flickering of a candle
To lights in full array.

God hangs the stars that sparkle
Across the evening sky,
Myriads of tiny lights
To light our world on high.

The chink of light that shines
Through a door that is ajar
Brings assurance and comfort
When from home afar.

For to live in darkness.
Is not a happy place!
Living in the light
Brings a special grace.

Light also helps us see.
The evils darkness hide
It helps us walk the walk
With goodness by our side.

So do not shun its presence
It will help you cope,
Revel in its presence
Fear will turn to hope.

BROKEN PIECES

Do we take our brokenness
Into our bright new morn!
Do we come weighed down
To greet another dawn?

Shards of sorrow
With jagged edge
Battle scars
We keep upon a ledge.

Sometimes we take them down,
Give them a little dust
Then we put them back
Why leave them there to rust?

Why can't we leave them
In the mists of yesteryear?
Why do we struggle with their weight?
Why do we fear?

They are the past,
Sharp and full of pain,
Leave them behind,
Don't live them all again!

Sometimes like shattered glass
Our memories are broken.
They can be restored
They are more than just a token.

It may take an act of will
Much shedding of tears
Cast away the baggage,
Which belongs to yesteryears.

Each new day we're given
Brings the message of new life,
A slate wiped clean.
A fresh story we can write.

Forgiveness may be the melody
Perhaps we have to sing
To things we cannot change
It is sad to try to cling.

Mercy will fall
Just like the gentle rain
When the brokenness has left
Our hearts are free again.

CARNIVAL CLOWN

You joke - you laugh
You smile - You frown.
How do you feel my Carnival Clown?
Is it a heart of stone you hide
As you join the crowd on
The carousel ride
Is it just a mask you wear?
To cover all the pain that's there?

Oh! My clown I want to know
If all that mirth is real or show.
Perhaps one day that mask you'll drop,
Still I can wait
Till the carnival stops.

THE GREAT I AM

You are the light in my window,
My bright and morning star
My warm glow of love
I worship from afar.

You are my candle shedding light
On life and all it brings,
You tell me you delight in me
My heart sings.

You are my door
I need but knock
You're there to bid me enter
Your promises unlock.

You are my bread of life
You nourish and sustain;
My spirit you replenish
My life a sweet refrain.

My cup is overflowing
With your Kingdom wine,
We are the many branches
You are the one true Vine.

No more my life
Is shifting sand
My feet upon a rock are set
You lead me by the hand.

Like Eagle wings you shelter
My spirit sealed in love
A serenade of hope
Comes from your heart above.

You are the way in which I walk
My steps you gently guide
In all I do you're there for me
You're walking by my side.

The Shepherd of your flock you are
I thank you I'm a part
Of that great family, whom have
Given you their heart

Help us never to forget
You are the great "I Am,"
Yet you became for us
The sacrificial Lamb.

You are the Resurrection and the Life
The message Easter sings
Your Holy Spirit our great gift
The power and joy you bring.

We're on the other side of Love,
Our Easter World is bright
Forgive us for our apathy
We ask for your great light.

So in this world divided
Sometimes our light grows dim,
Shine brightly in my window
Keep me strong within!

THE SILENT TIMES

It's the silent times I love
When all the world is still.
My thoughts can freely wander
And linger where they will.

The busy-ness has ceased
The noise has quickly fled
At last I sit and ponder
Reflect on what's been said.

The tensions of the day
Have vanished with the light
The evening hour is tranquil
As I lift my pen to write.

A process of relinquishing
The hurts incurred this day
The angry words unbidden
I never meant to say.

A joy to savour sweetly
Time with a friend I've spent
Her never failing honesty
Her listening ear she lent.

To place into perspective,
The worries of each child
Viewed from this silent hour
They're somehow rather mild.

A time to dream those wondrous dreams
That challenge us to more,
To grow in life's great song
It's symphony restore.

How I need this silent hour
To pray and work things through
To look to God, at world and self
Tomorrow's day I'll greet anew.

AFTERNOON REFLECTIONS

Afternoon Reflections.
Soft sea breeze blows gently
And steals across my face.

Surfboards tipped at crazy angles
As homeward bound they race,
Children playing happily
Sand castles built so high.

While far above a lonesome kite
Is flying to the sky
Sun and sand surround me
In a blanket so secure.
I want to stop forever
It calls me on to more.

THOUGHT

When I am flying high Lord...
Help me to land safely.

Ramblings

SURROGACY - CHRISTMAS THOUGHTS

This morning I am reflecting on a mother of three, who in a wonderful spirit of generosity has shared her ability to bear a child with a friend who does not have that blessing.

That life already growing within her, she will cherish and bring to birth and in a great act of love will present this little new life to the biological parents. Surrogacy is a word of life to many, some may question the ethics and morality it may pose.

This Christmas I am reflecting also on another Mother! Could Mary, the Mother of our Lord, chosen before the Beginning of time be our first example of Surrogacy? Did she know that her Mother-Father God of the Universe, Creator of all would choose her to bring His son to birth? His only child nurtured in the womb of a young woman.

A woman of her time who would have faced the disapproval and morality of that day. One who could give herself so generously - who could praise in the beautiful words of what we now know as the Magnificat.
    " My soul does praise the Lord
    And my spirit does rejoice in God my Saviour."

Then in the fulness of time she gave Him back to His Father, and in so doing He saved and blessed us forever.
THANK YOU MARY!
And thank you to that unnamed friend who will also bring the gift of life. We rejoice with you.

KAY'S ISOLATION RAMBLINGS - APRIL 19, 2020

Hello dear friends,

How are things going with our isolation, social distancing etc.? I have to say that we are faring pretty well. Our freezer is still looking very healthy and groaning with delight at all the goodies that are coming our way. It is very handy having children who live close by and who are all pretty good cooks. Merry and Andrew called in today with lasagne which we have had for dinner this evening and also brought three other meals for the freezer. Alison also has been cooking for us, or perhaps it may have been Julian as he also is an excellent cook. Alison rings us a few times a week and asks do we have a shopping list. And David and Mika have brought some lovely casseroles and soup. They are really looking after us. I feel guilty sometimes, as I am capable of cooking. However some evenings when I have had a not so good day it is helpful to open the freezer and choose what we want and pop it in the Microwave, so I have decided it is not so bad after all to be classed as elderly and vulnerable.

Not that any of us really see ourselves fitting into that description. It's strange isn't it that we never feel inside that we are the age we are. It is our body that lets us down!

I have digressed a little (nothing new for me.) I began this email yesterday afternoon. It is now Sunday morning about 6.45am. We will be going to virtual church this morning - not far to walk - just the lounge room. Then at 11.30 am we will be having our morning tea as we always do after our service. This is virtual, as it will be using Zoom. Interesting! This pandemic is certainly introducing us to new ways of doing things.

I have heard several folk, commentators and the like, saying that when this pandemic is no longer with us that as a society we are going to be changed, more compassionate, not as materialistic etc. I wonder!!!

Also every day I seem to be receiving emails with all sorts of conspiracy theories rolled out. It is amazing when anything happens untoward in our society, the speed that our imaginations go to work. Just look at all the clever skits etc that the Internet is flooded with. Some are quite brilliant.

I think dear friends, I need to draw this to a close after all, I do have to consult with my wardrobe to see what outfit I can wear to my virtual church service. I have a friend who also goes to an online service who dresses in her very best and posts photos on face book. I won't be doing that, however I admire her spirit. She is determined that this lockdown will not get the better of her.

Much love to you all and as one friend wrote. "Keep your pecker up" meaning keep your chin up in other words, keep cheerful. Take care and keep safe.
xxxx
Kay

PONDERINGS ON REFUGEES!

I am recalling that Jesus said in the Gospels, "When you do it unto the least of these you do it unto me!" I think we all know the context of this verse. He is pointing out that when we show mercy and help our neighbour, it is as if we do it to Jesus himself. Mind blowing isn't it? It beggars the question... Are we who call ourselves Christians becoming desensitized to the teachings of Jesus?

Is this a societal thing? I guess what started me on this train of thought was an issue that many of us hold dear to our heart. That is the seemingly complex question of our refugees, and our government's way of dealing with it. I know that we as Christians come from many and varied backgrounds, have been subject to different teachings, and obviously do not share the same views on certain aspects of our faith. We don't all have the same passions. Even so there are some things that perhaps we could become more passionate about. If not so, perhaps we could least try and understand what this verse is saying to us.

As I sat reflecting on this, it seemed to me that we could look at this almost in terms of us being a huge pastoral care group. This is just not for individuals, however Jesus is calling each one to do, something for him. That something happens to be caring for his people, you and I and caring for each other. It may take the form perhaps of visiting a prison, a hospital, a refugee centre, feeding and help to care for the aged and the homeless. Or perhaps it may be dealing with things that come along in our church or neighbourhood. No matter how big or small we are doing it for Him.

However what about our attitudes especially to our refugees? Many of us feel the frustration of wanting to help, but find it almost impossible to do so. It is hard to argue with very fixed government policies. One often feels as if you are banging your head against a brick wall. What would Jesus do?

I'm sure that He would not do what we are seeing both our political parties do. It is hard to reconcile the thought that some of our leaders are Christians, yet feel what is happening is an OK thing. Is it out of sight out of mind? How can that be when so many folk in our community are agitating for change! Perhaps there are not enough of us. What do we have to do to get their attention? When you meet refugees and hear their stories... When you actually put a face to what you see and hear in the media...how can your attitude not change?

I wish I had the answer! Is it that we need to pray more? Perhaps we should be praying more intentionally for our Government, for our leaders, especially those involved in Immigration and our Prime Minister that the Spirit of God might bring a softening of hearts and attitudes.

I must confess that I become so angry when I think about it all, that I feel very little love for our governing bodies. I guess I am thinking about them as the enemy, and after all God's mandate to us is also to pray for and love our enemies.

This whole question has no easy answer, however when I read this part of the gospel, it seems to be speaking very clearly about what our role should be. I am reminded of Louisa Toogood, who some of you will know of or may have met. She is no longer with us. However about 45 years ago she was challenged by this very verse (the one above), which led to her starting the Ecumenical Coffee Brigade, which is still serving the homeless and the poor in the streets of Brisbane.

She was a great lady, much loved by those she served. To hear her story is very encouraging. I first met her about 40 or so years ago when the work was quite young, and for many years, probably about 25... took part in a sandwich-cutting roster in the early morning. One thing that really stands in my mind is her relating how God challenged her with this particular verse.

It was her custom to attend the morning service at the cathedral. Driving through the city in that early hour she would often see homeless folk on the street. She would feel the niggling of the Holy Spirit. The day came when God confronted her in no uncertain terms. As she walked back in to her city flat, it was as if that verse was written across her living room wall. God had spoken, and Louisa obeyed. She was 69 years old and retired! How she started the work, and what happened in the ensuing years is another story!

I'm not quite sure what has led me to reflect on this. Perhaps it is Jesus challenging my own attitudes. Let us pray for one another, for our friends and enemies!!   Amen

MEANDERINGS

Just recently a lovely friend shared with me her thought for the day. It came from the writings of Hans Christian Anderson. This is what he said:

"JUST LIVING IS NOT ENOUGH, ONE MUST HAVE FREEDOM, SUNSHINE AND A LITTLE FLOWER."

These are very basic aren't they? Things that I guess that you and I take for granted each day that we are given. We walk in freedom, most days we have glorious sunshine, and well, the little flower is the icing on the cake.

What if we did not have these things? My mind immediately flies to our refugees, who are still in detention! Can you imagine being incarcerated in a place like Nauru, Manus or even one of the onshore centres, which are prisons where people are treated as criminals.

When we realise that some of these folk have been shut away for a number of years, without opportunity to experience even the most basic joys of living, our hearts should be crying! Can we understand their fragility of spirit? Hope has been taken from them. They are broken people.

Even if the sun is shining. They do not feel its warmth. They do not feel the sense of awe as it rises over the sea to banish the darkness of the long night. Likewise they do not see the wonder of it painting its vibrant hues as it slowly sets in the West.

'Freedom' is a word they think about constantly, the freedom to be the people they really are. Not to be hidden behind lock and key! To be able to sit in a cafe with a cup of coffee or to just go shopping. Things we do every day without even thinking of what a privilege we are enjoying.

As for the little flower - a wonder of our natural creation. To hold the beauty of a flower in our hand is special. An affirmation from our creator. He has given us freedom to walk in sunshine to warm our spirit, and then in love he gives us a sign.

I love to be given flowers, to have flowers in the house.
I long for the day when our refugee brothers and sisters will know all these same pleasures. I have this picture in my mind, I see them not just living but walking free, the sunshine warming their backs, in their hands a flower!

THE YEAR OF THE GRANDMOTHER
(SOME EARLY REFLECTIONS)

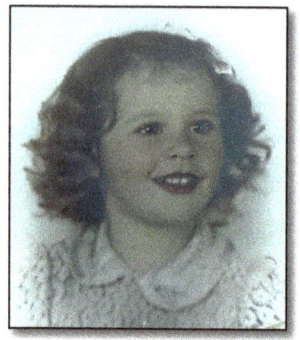

15. Kay at age five.

It was my first year of school! We lived in a small country coastal village although village is probably not the word to use. We were one of about five houses facing a beach, which stretched along the east coast of the country as far as the eye could see. The year was 1945, the war was ending and I was about to start school.

We were a small family of four, my brother little more than a baby. The nearest school was some miles away so my mother decided to send me to live with her mother, my nana for that first school year! Nana lived in a small village on the banks of the Tweed River, NSW. As my mind travels back over the years, I marvel at how many people actually lived in that small house.

There was my grandmother and grandfather, (Nana and Pa), there was my Uncle Bob, their unmarried son, Auntie Dot, their single daughter, Uncle Joe, my grandfather's brother, Uncle Johnny, my Nana's brother. They were the blood relatives, however then there was Mrs Holmes, affectionately known to me as "Holmsie."

16. Grandmother and Holmsie.

"Holmsie" was about the same age as my grandmother. She was Swedish, and had quite an accent. It seems she and her husband had lived close by and their home had burnt to the ground. They had been taken in by Nana, by the time I remember her, she had lost her husband and was living there on her own.

How we all fitted is rather mind boggling, however we did! I shared a double bed with "Holmsie," which I thought nothing of. In those days this was often done. The house was highset with four small bedrooms on the top level, plus the bed on the verandah, which was quite a common feature. Downstairs, sort of bunkhouse style was the area allotted to Joe and Johnny.

To a five year old this was all quite exciting. Mealtimes we all sat around the big old table. Fish was served in great abundance, as the men of the family had a small fishing business, and bearing in mind that these had been war years, many foods were not that plentiful! Poor Uncle Johnny used to have great trouble eating fish. Many the times he would sit in panic with a bone lodged in his throat whilst Nana hovered near by with chunks of bread ready to help the offensive bone on its way.

Next door but one was the little country pub. Here Aunty Dot worked in the bar. I used to think that she was so sophisticated as I would sit on the bed watching her prepare for her evening out! I guess at the time she was probably about 20, however to my childish eyes she was such a wonderful woman of the world. I would watch, wide eyed as sitting in front of my Nana's old fashioned dressing table firstly she would roll her hair in the style of the day. Then came the make up. Even after all these years, I can still smell the perfume she would splash around liberally! Even today it is capable of evoking those long ago memories.

On reflection apart from those times, I don't remember Auntie Dot being around that much. I guess, like all young girls she had her own social life, and after all I was a five-year old kid!

Her brother Bob was a taciturn young man, whom I recall seeing little of apart from his presence at the meal table. I think I sort of kept out of his way. Uncle Joe, like my grandfather was a bluff, happy man, who seemed to be quite relaxed with the presence of a child in the house.

The men of the family spent most of the day out on the water fishing. It was a common sight to walk down the road and see them mending their nets on the riverbank, the pungent scent of tar hanging heavily in the morning air.

On looking back it seems that my grandmother was akin to the managing director. I still recall her packing the catch of the day in the large downstairs cold room, killing crabs and the like. It seemed that folk deferred to her. One thing that I always felt strange, although it of course was typical of the day was how she and Mrs. Holmes, who had been friends for many years still called each other Mrs, never Bella and Ida! Nana was very strait laced in many ways. Did not like young girls to wear shorts etc. However would every Saturday have a bet on the horses, and sit glued to the wireless all afternoon.

As I write this I am beginning to wonder what it must have been like to have her granddaughter to care for as well as all the rest of her extended family. I was the first grandchild, however a year later my mother's older sister Hilda produced a baby girl. Because she was close to my age, it often happened that we two cousins occupied the verandah bed.

How different those times were! Often as we sat on the verandah we would see a swagman carrying his swag trudging along the road. I can remember feeling a bit afraid at first, however after the first few encounters they became part of the local scenery.

The local area was known for its sugar cane plantations with the sugar mill just being a few miles up river. Often we would sit on the riverbank and watch the barge as it transported the cane to the mill. This was greatly exciting to we kids as often we would be the recipients of pieces of cane thrown from the boat which we would sit and suck all afternoon. The sickly sweet juice I can taste as I write.

The little village hall was used for many community get-togethers. Nana and her friends would go to the local dances. Not to dance, however to play Euchre with all the other like minded folk in the area behind the dance floor. I used to be taken along, sat on a chair to watch the adults dancing. However the highlight of the evening would be when supper was served! Huge big tea kettles would be brought out, the tea poured and then big slabs of cake handed around!

Another treat was the pineapple man! At regular intervals he would appear at the door carrying a large basket of tiny pineapples. To this day I cannot recall a pineapple that was sweeter. We would slice off the top and scoop the contents out with a spoon. Fruit was always plentiful. Sitting under the Mango trees, we would eat mangoes until our tummies ached, and our clothes were so juicy and sticky, we were almost ready to be thrown in the bath. Cherry Guavas were another favourite. The tree was always abundantly blessed with fruit.

The grocery store another experience so far removed from our supermarkets of today. I still see Mr. Pritchard standing behind that timber counter dressed in a white apron, a pencil behind his ear and a notebook at the ready with which to add up the bill. Very little at that time was packaged. The flour, sugar etc. would be scooped out into brown paper bags. I used to love those errands to the grocery store as always I would be given a penny, or if I was lucky a halfpenny to buy a lolly with.

In the lane around the corner from the store was the village baker. The bakery itself was half open air. Can you imagine the wonderful aroma. There is nothing like the smell of freshly cooked bread to play havoc with one's taste buds. By the time the big black-crusted bread arrived home it would have the evidence of little fingers that just could not overcome temptation.

Down by the grocery store was the old ferry, which of course, today has been superseded by a modern bridge. However at that time the ferry was the only way of reaching those folk who lived on the other side of the river. A little further on was the Presbytery where an order of nuns lived. I can recall being greatly fascinated by these ladies in their strange black habits. I think I was always somewhat in awe of them!

Then of course the reason why I was living that year with my Grandmother - the school! The school itself was set in an open field with the schoolmaster's house adjoining. I, being in the Kindergarten class (Actually I think we called it first class,) had a young lady teacher.

The rest of the school was taught by the headmaster. Rows of desks, each row for a different class! With the same set up applying to the blackboard, the work neatly written in chalk for each class.
Of course they were the days of the old wooden desks with inkwells, and scratchy pens. That would come later for me at the next country school I attended. I guess being the littlies in the school, pencils were the order of the day. I was probably quite spoilt, as every day Nana would arrive at lunchtime with my little pack of sandwiches. None of this peanut butter and vegemite! The menu of the day would be crab, or fresh pineapple, this was made easier by the fact that the school was literally around the corner from where our house was.

One of my young friends from those school days, whom I had not seen or heard of for well over 60 years I was to meet again. This time, both 70 plus and where did we meet? In that same village hall at an anniversary celebration! What a thrill that was!

One of the joys that I remember quite clearly was the school fancy dress ball, my very first dress up occasion and I a bride no less, in full regalia. My hair was wrapped in rags to produce those lovely

Shirley Temple curls. I was so pleased with how I looked. (I still have the photo tucked away.)

I have always had a fascination with dolls. During the war, they were quite expensive. I have fond memories of the black doll, which my mother made for me. I can still see her in her green check gingham dress with her little tufts of pink hair. Today I guess she would be quite politically incorrect. You can imagine my euphoria when I discovered that my grandmother's next-door neighbour had a beautiful doll. And Joy of joys, I was invited to come in many times just so I could hold her. She was very special and kept in a glass cabinet. Also she was quite large. I would be instructed to sit on a chair, and then she would be very carefully put into my arms. I was in seventh heaven. How I longed for a doll just like that. To this day my love affair with dolls remains. If you would walk into my home you would find a plethora of them. Dolls, dolls, dolls, all shapes and sizes, sitting on chairs, reclining on beds, perched on cupboards. Strangely enough neither of our two daughters shared this same passion.

Around the corner from the school was the little Presbyterian Church. Every Sunday morning religiously I was sent off to Sunday school. This for me was the highlight of my week. Each Sunday we would be told a story, sing some choruses and then be sent home armed with our little cards with the text for the day. I loved collecting all those cards. Even now I hold them in my memory, pretty pastel colours, dainty illustrations of birds and flowers. Later down the track and living back with my family, I was sent to the local Church of England Sunday school. I never liked the stamps we were given there nearly as much as those little text cards.

Looking back on those early days of Sunday school I realise that even at that young age a foundation was being laid upon which my faith in later life would be built. Of course I was not old enough to hear any great theological truths, however more importantly I was to understand in my childish way what the love of God meant. We had a middle-aged lady, I recall Miss Flavell as if I was sitting in her class now. She was the kindest person. If you asked me, I probably would not be able to recall one thing that she taught us. However there was no need, her very attitude and her love for each one of us was sufficient. She had the wonderful gift of just "being" Perhaps this is something that we need more of today. My heart is grateful.

As I write this I find I am recollecting things that I had almost forgotten. At that time we would have on local radio funeral notices. I recall that they would engender in me a feeling of inexorable sadness. It mattered little that I was in no way connected to the departed folk, each time I would hear that special music followed by the announcement a wave of sadness would engulf me. I would just hope I would never have to listen to any of my family. I guess at that age death was an unknown and thinking about it was not easy.

My memories of my grandfather are a little hazy. To me looking back he was more of a shadowy figure in the background. It was the age of decisive roles for men and for women. Women's work was one thing and men's another. Pa (as I called him) could often be found in the old kitchen sitting at the table. Sometimes he would play his violin. He did not live a long life and died a few years after I had left the house.

That year was a special year. It seems that for some reason I collected more memories than I did in the years before and after.

About three years later our family moved to the city, returning once a year to holiday with my grandmother. New experiences were to follow. And now I am growing old and perhaps somewhat nostalgic. However I give thanks for, "The Year Of The Grandmother"

17. Kay's teddy bear tea party

18. Grandmother's house

FRIENDS RAMBLINGS

Good morning dear friends,

I think it is time for another early morning ramble. That makes it sound as if it may be a trifle incoherent, however I will try to write as logically as I can!

So much seems to have happened since my last missive that I don't quite know where to start. Perhaps this is a good place, I came across this in facebook recently - *"We have Art so that we shall not die of Reality,"* a little quote by the German philosopher Friedrich Nietzsche. I think when we look at the world around us and the news that greets our eyes each time we turn our televisions on, we could really embrace this same thought. Reality does leave a lot to be desired and art in all its various forms is a welcome intrusion.

We have so many artistic and creative people not only in our world but just within our own circle of friends and I'm sure most of us could echo the same thing. We have to remember also that art is not just using one medium such as oils or watercolours from which beautiful pictures are created. However there are many ways in which we can express our creativity.

Many years ago Edith Schaeffer who together with her husband and family lived in a Christian community called L'Abri in the Swiss Alps, wrote a book called Hidden Art, which speaks of the various creative gifts that we have been given. If you are like me and always wishing that you had some great artistic talent, instead of being someone who can hardly colour in without going over the lines, this is certainly a book that you would enjoy. There are so many things that we can do which in our everyday life we take for granted, it may be taking the time to set a table beautifully which makes guests feel welcomed, and loved. Although having said that I can recall a time when my daughters were in their teens and it was their turn to have the church youth group meeting and supper at our house. I fussed about as most mothers do setting the table nicely with flowers etc as a centrepiece. Was it appreciated? No! In fact, quite the opposite. My girls told me that wasn't what anyone else does etc. etc. So much for my little bit of art.

This morning I read a beautiful love story. Some 25 years ago a villager from a small village in Croatia stumbled upon a wounded stork that had been shot by hunters and could no longer fly. He adopted her, cared for her and even built a nest for her on his own rooftop. He named her Malena. Five years passed then a remarkable thing happened. A male stork landed in Malena's nest one day after making the long migration from Africa. He became her mate. Even though she could not fly they became bonded for life. The villager named the male stork Klepetan. Every year Klepetan flies 8,000 miles to reunite with his wounded soul mate. Such a lovely story, it almost brought tears to my eyes. Sometimes the lives of birds and animals in nature are quite extraordinary. Aren't they?
With love,
Kay xx

19. Pair of Storks

RAMBLINGS ON LIGHT

Dear Friends,
Today is a bright and sunny day in Brisbane. I love the sunshine it lifts my spirits and everything seems much happier than when we have dull and gloomy days. When I was a child I can remember really disliking the darkness, in fact I was rather afraid. When my mother put me to bed I always had the door a little ajar so I could have a chink of light shining in from the hallway. Even now I don't like to be in the wholly dark and we have lights that we always leave on, although of course these days it is for the practical purpose of nocturnal trips to the bathroom.

LET THERE BE LIGHT
While we are on the subject of light, you may remember that last year I took part in a three months trial conducted by the Mater hospital and the University of Qld using laser light therapy for Parkinson's. We were supposed to have the results about six months ago however they still have not surfaced. From memory I think Australia is the only country to date, which has been carrying out serious trials for the use of low level laser light for PD. However this time I think it may be my last option for pain management for my knee, I still think about the stem cell treatment and keep up to date via the worldwide stem cell face book group to which I belong. However it is very problematic and the FDA has closed a lot of clinics in the U.S. Also it is very expensive with no guaranteed results.

Originally I had intended to see a doctor whom I found was practising it here in his clinic, however on reflection I think I can do it myself. I think I may have mentioned that about ten years ago, Merry, our Vet daughter decided that she would buy the laser and try it in her vet practice. For some reason she never got around to using it, so I am now the sole owner of this little wand, which I'm hoping to be able to learn how to use. It comes with a video and a book and works as acupuncture does on your pressure points. There is very little information about the length of time to use it etc.

I am thinking I will take the email address of the Vet who has invented the system and see if I can email him for some more information. I am just hoping he is still with us as the last time I embarked on a similar exercise I found that the gentleman in question had been dead for three years. Let there be Light!

Light figures in so much of our life, doesn't it. The biblical writers used it to illustrate a lot of their sayings. Jesus used it in his parables, etc. We are asked to be light in someone's darkness.

I once read there is a crack in everything. That is how the light gets in. Here is another find from Facebook, I love this one - it speaks of our brokenness seen in a positive light.

> "No one is perfect, however that very fact means that our lives count, that out of our cracks and broken pieces can come something beautiful. We can learn to light a candle in the darkest moments of someone's life."

Thank you to all of you, my lovely friends who continue to light a candle in so many ways for me. In one of the churches to which we have belonged over the years we had the opportunity to light a candle. We usually did it after coming forward for communion. I loved this practice. I could pray for some situations, as I lit the candle bringing them into the presence of God. I love all the symbolism, it helps me to focus.

With love and gratitude, Kay Xx

PALM SUNDAY RAMBLINGS - APRIL 2020

Good morning dear friends,

It is 2:30am, Palm Sunday, the beginning of Holy week.
This morning there will be no palms tied to the pews in our churches, nor a stream of church members processing down the Aisle carrying palm fronds as they re-enact Jesus entering Jerusalem. Instead the churches will be empty, and the faithful will be watching a service online.

I am feeling sad. Easter to me and most Christians is the most important Festival on the church Calendar. I have many lovely memories of this special time. We were often in Noosa for the Palm Sunday celebration. For some years we held our service in the park on the Banks of the Noosa River. We would all gather together each with a palm frond and make our way waving our fronds in to our outdoor Cathedral. It was early morning, the service was 7.30 am, a lovely time for worship. The air was fresh, the sun newly risen, the river as yet undisturbed, tranquil it would just seem as if the whole world was at peace.

Of course we knew that that was not the case, but for a moment in time it became so. Perhaps as we worship this morning whether on line or perhaps in our own little family service, we too can find that moment to put aside the sad and tragic happenings in our world family and come together in praise and thanksgiving, it is not that we have forgotten our sadnesses or our prayers for the healing of our world.

Perhaps we need to turn away from the incessant chatter of the television and other forms of media, give ourselves a little time out, using it for stillness and reflection. In whichever way we choose to worship, and for some it may just be sitting quietly with our thoughts, we are all different and that is ok!
We send our blessings and love.

MY JOURNEY WITH PARKINSON'S - PART 1 - 2013

I'm not quite sure why I'm putting pen to paper, perhaps it will be therapeutic for me to do so. Perhaps, and I'm hoping that this will be the case someone out there may be asking some of the questions I have asked. Or may be experiencing similar symptoms.

I feel that I would like to share some of the insights I have gained over these dozen years or so as I have walked this precarious road.

Before diagnosis I knew very little about Parkinson's. I had first encountered it during the many years that I had volunteered with Meals on Wheels. One of our clients comes vividly to mind. I can still see this older gentleman standing in his kitchen shaking with a very extreme tremor whilst we cut up his food for him. He was so miserable and to this day I still feel the sadness that I felt for him each time we brought his meal.

My next encounter was with my own father. My mother had died some five years earlier and dad was now living on his own in another city. For some time he had suffered with a bad tremor, however most of us, as he was over eighty attributed this to advancing age. On one of our regular visits I persuaded him to go to his GP for a check up. I drew the doctors attention to my father's tremor. His response was to ask him to hold his hands out in front of him and then say in quite a casual manner, "You have a bit of the Parkinson's, I'll give you some pills". Full stop! That was it - no explanations, no referrals to a neurologist or anyone else for that matter.

Dad was from the old school - doctors were gods, you never questioned them, they had spoken and that was it. A few months later when I returned to see him, I asked how the medication was going, "Oh!" He said, "I'm not taking it any more. It wasn't helping me so I decided not to use it." It was not until he finally went into assisted living accommodation with a new doctor and someone to oversee his medication that he was actually taking it on a regular basis.

When I look back now with the benefit of my own experience and knowledge, I really feel sad that I did not know more then. My knowledge was probably even less than that of the average lay person now. In those days I did not have computer, iPad, or any other digital help - that all came later. One of the things that I do remember with shame was the unpleasant drooling that dad had that is common to a lot of Parkinson's sufferers, we never realised that and were constantly chiding him. We could have helped him if only we had known the cause of it. I guess the experience we had with dad is not uncommon. I certainly can identify with it.

I was experiencing symptoms for at least two years before I was finally diagnosed. If you are also a PD sufferer, I know that most of you will identify with the frustration of this. As we know PD is a very individual disease. We suffer from many different symptoms, we are unique. My first symptom that I really noticed was difficulty in taking a deep breath. After consulting with my GP, I began a round of tests, specialists etc. I saw respiratory doctors, cardiologists, specialist physicians, ear nose and throat doctors, had tests, scans etc. etc. During this time I was also sent to a neurologist as I was having some trouble walking. There were times when my legs just did not want to move. I could no longer get on a chair to reach something from a high cupboard and I was feeling quite uncomfortable when walking. The neurologist gave me a good going over, did nerve tests, which apparently showed some irregularity, he assured me I did not have Parkinson's, MS, or any other serious neurological problem and advised me to go to the gym for three months.

The physician said he thought I had a type of asthma, and tried me on puffers etc. all to no avail. As for my inability to climb on the chair etc, he demonstrated that he could do it, and seeing that we were roughly the same age, why couldn't I do it? Precisely the question that I was asking him. As I look back I realise that everyone I saw thought they had some answer, however unfortunately no one was looking at the whole picture. By this time my GP had put me on Zoloft thinking that it might help with the breathing. I stopped on this for nine months however my symptoms rather than decreasing were growing worse. Twice I was admitted to emergency with my breathing problems. The first time, nothing was found. I seemed to have enough oxygen in my blood though struggling hard to get it. The second time, to my annoyance and disappointment the young Doctor on duty told me that there was absolutely nothing wrong with me and that I needed to see a good counsellor. I came home, as you can imagine feeling quite depressed.

About this time, my GP who had tried so hard to help me left the practice and moved interstate. It was a good opportunity to find another GP who could look at my problems with the objectivity of fresh vision. By this time I was really coming to the conclusion that in fact I did have PD even though that had been ruled out by the neurologist. By this time I was having trouble with my voice also. People were remarking how soft it had become, and in a group which I belonged to at that time, when it was my turn to read, I would always ask the person next to me to read for me.

The GP I found sent me for various blood tests. When writing the request, I asked him could he include one for Parkinson's. With my limited knowledge I did not know that there was not a test which could determine the diagnosis. He told me this, however did not ask why I had requested it etc, something which he later apologised for. After three weeks of talking and test taking we were no further advanced. As he saw me to the door on that last consultation I turned to him and said, "don't you think that you should send me to a Neurologist? With great surprise he said "What for?" So sitting back down, I told him what is suspected and why. I reminded him that on my initial visit I had requested a test for Parkinson's. He apologised for not picking up my concern at that time. After much talking, examining my gait etc. he conceded that it could be a real possibility. He then referred me to a neurologist whom he said was a good diagnostician and also a movement disorder specialist.

Finally after three months of uncomfortable and anxious waiting I was sitting in the neurologist's office. With very little talking and a brief exam, without hesitation, he pronounced that in fact I had PD. I was surprised that he had reached that decision so quickly and remarked on it. He replied that he knew almost at once from observing me in the waiting room. He congratulated me on getting my diagnosis correct.

I have to say that receiving this news in a lot of ways was a relief. I could now put a name to this group of symptoms, and having a name meant I could fight it! Of course there were a gamut of emotions, especially in those early days. Loss and grief for the lifestyle I was losing etc. I was floundering a lot, as the neurologist had told me very little apart from giving me the script for the medication (Madopar 125. 100mg) to be taken three times a day, and advising me not to join a support group as it would depress me beyond belief.

Although I now had this diagnosis, the neurologist was quite adamant that my breathing problems had nothing to do with PD. I could not accept this as apart from being the first symptom I had, it was certainly relieved by the medication. Each time I visited him, he would insist that I was not correct in my thinking re this symptom. Finally the time came when I was able to visit Google and start my search to arm myself with as much information that I could. I was not content to sit back and let this disease have control of me. In fact, every morning I would sit on the side of the bed and talk to it, telling it, it was not going to be part of my life! (just as well there were no flies on the wall.)

The first thing I did was purchase a book written by an authority on Parkinson's in the U.S. As I read through, I found that indeed my breathing problems were related to PD as well of course much other useful information. I firmly believe that we all need to acquaint ourselves with as much information as we possibly can. Of course we need the skill of our doctors as well, and ideally their support, however for many of us that does not happen, and after all no one will care for our body the way we do. We owe it to ourselves!

Even with this written confirmation my neurologist would not believe or admit that my breathing was in anyway linked to my PD. I even took the book to show him, however he refused to look, commenting that the book was obviously wrong. Finally in desperation I sought a second opinion from a well-known, well thought of neurologist who confirmed that indeed it was. My doctor then accepted it, with the not so gracious comment, " you are the first patient whom I have ever seen with this symptom."
Not withstanding the fact that I had been told previously that all PD patients were different and could exhibit a variety of symptoms, no two people being exactly the same!

One of the reasons which prompted me to have a second opinion was that some months earlier I had had a time of poor breathing and felt so miserable that I went to my husband's GP to see if he may have been able to give me some relief. When I explained to him it was one of my PD symptoms he refuted it. He got out his book from his drawer opened it up and reeled off about four of the well known symptoms - tremor, bradikynesia, rigidity of muscles etc. and then with almost an air of triumph said, "What you have is anxiety...very common in women of your age!" Finished this off with, " why don't you admit it, you need to see a good counsellor!" That was the last time I ever visited that particular G.P.

Now my search was in earnest to find help. Prayer has always been an important part of my life, I know that many friends pray regularly for me, this is a great comfort knowing that whatever else I do that I am being supported in this way. For some who may be reading this, prayer may not be something that you use. I think to have a positive attitude is of major importance, and always to have hope, is something that we can all employ.

In those early days I found a group called Parkinson's Recovery in the U.S. I subscribed to them and am still receiving their Emails, telling me what is happening. Their weekly radio programs, which I access, have guests whom I always find interesting, folk who are using different modalities in order to help their symptoms. It was a guest on that program who spoke on the benefit of Qi gong, which had helped her tremendously. This encouraged me to find a teacher in my home city who put me on the right track and now I try use her DVD's on a regular basis.

I found a Speech Therapist who helped me with exercises to improve my voice, which was also helpful. Another friend told me about the Butayko breathing course, which I also did. For me personally searching and finding avenues of help was the means of keeping hope alive. I did find that the first five years lived up pretty well to the book's description of those years being called the "Honey Moon" period.

My PD was not restricting me a great deal. Medication was helpful and my husband and I did much overseas travelling.

My searching the Internet continued. I found an organisation in the UK called Viartis, which regularly sends me the news of all the research being undertaken and what the results are. It is purely factual with no bias.

Our overseas trips continued. Our very good friend in the UK whom we visited regularly is a retired Doctor. Sadly her partner, about five years after I had my diagnosis was diagnosed with PD as well. When there we would share information with each other. Sadly after a few years it was realised that her partner was atypical Parkinson's, and subsequently diagnosed with MSA. Consequently because of this, I became quite familiar with the symptoms of both MSA and PSP.

I then heard the benefits of mindfulness, so again consulted Google and found a course, which was about to start in my area. I enjoyed this and try to use it in my daily life. My balance was not that good so I found a physio, who specialised in that area and did the course, which entailed quite a bit of exercise to be done at home.

About this time I became interested in learning more of a drug, which I am sure many of you have heard of called Low Dose Naltrexone, (LDN). Some years before I had read the book called " Up the creek with a Paddle" written by Mary Anne Boyle Bradley at that time my medication was working quite well, and I guess I filed it away somewhere in the recesses of my brain to be recalled at another time.

It was through another guest on the Parkinson's recovery program that I heard it spoken of again. A PD patient had tried it and was finding it very helpful. She spoke at length on that particular program of its benefits. I emailed her for more information, and then read as many reports as I could about it. It was worth a go - next to no side effects, inexpensive, I figured that even if it didn't help me it could not hurt me so I resolved to give it a go.

This was easier said than done. My G.P. would not prescribe it. He said that after consulting with his colleagues he had decided against it as they said it was rubbish! My neurologist would not help either. So back to Google where I found a chap who was on it who gave me the name of a doctor who by chance lived in this area and was very happy to supply me with scripts. It requires a compounding pharmacy to dispense it. I send mine to a pharmacy in Adelaide, which was recommended to me. Apparently it is very important that the correct filler is used.

Since then I have joined the LDN Trust which is based in the U.K. and receive lots of information re: trials etc. and helpful videos, testaments from those who are using it, plus, interviews from various medicos around the world who are using it for their patients. I have been using it for over three years and feel that it is helpful.

I also for the last three years have been having Bowen Therapy, once a fortnight, which has also been helpful.

Over the past few years much has been written on Neuroplasticity. I have purchased the two books written by Dr. Norman Doidge, and have read them with great interest, also the book on the same topic written by Barbara Arrowsmith Young. I also had the opportunity to hear her speak when she was visiting our city a couple of years ago. I have many books on my shelves purchased over the years, which have all added something to my understanding of PD. In fact it is a bit like buying the various books on weight loss. I always say if it is the number of books you read I should be as skinny as a rake. Possibly a bit the same with my little library of Parkinson related books, if it was reading that affected a cure, I would be bursting with health.

As the years have gone by my symptoms have became much more troublesome. From the outset I was determined to keep my medication to the minimum. Some would argue that this is the wrong thing to do. I have been told by doctors at times that I am under medicated. I have experimented with various dosages, and at the present remain on five (5) madopar daily, sometimes taking an extra one through the night. At present this seems to work for me as well. I take an LDN in the evening.

Some time ago I came across an excellent book that deals mainly with Medication written by J. Eric Ahlskog, PhD, MD called "The New Parkinson Disease Treatment book". He is from the Mayo Clinic and is a leading authority on PD. I have found it extremely helpful.

One important thing that I have realised is the necessity to be diligent with the taking of my medication and protein. I am very mindful of when I have eaten etc, in relation to taking my pill. I allow the one-hour after my meal, or otherwise take it half an hour before eating. Dr. Ahlskog in the above book is even stricter. He recommends one hour before meals, and 2 hours after eating.

Also it is important not to have aspartame, as it has the same protein in it that will inhibit the absorption of the medication. The latter was something that I had never been told. Now I am very careful due to the inability to swallow saliva when my pills are wearing off, I was chewing lots of gum, which in fact contained aspartame. I searched and found a gum in the pharmacy, which ticks all the boxes. It is a little expensive and a lot of pharmacies don't seem to stock it, however I usually buy enough to last me for a while. I haven't chewed gum since I was a child and never liked to see folk chewing, and here I am chewing most of the day. Ironic isn't it?

Of late there has been quite a bit of publicity both on Parkinson's sites and also in the media on the benefit of Dance. One of my friends goes regularly to dance for PD Ballet class and really enjoys that way of exercising. Also the tango is said to be very helpful and looks like a lot of fun.

About eighteen months ago I started having an hour weekly with a lovely personal trainer. He is familiar with PD and also neuroplasticity so is really helpful in explaining ways to help establish new neural pathways. He has given me a group of exercises, including breathing which I try to do every day. (Sometimes I fall short). However what I am really enjoying is that he is teaching me to tango! He needs a lot of patience, however I'm hopeful that one evening I will have mastered it sufficiently to be able to brave a dance floor. Also he is encouraging my positivity. I try hard in that area however it is at times not the easiest and we can all do with help.

For some reason I have found (and please note that this is just my own experience) that doctors when it comes to PD are lacking in positivity. Certainly I have never had any encouragement in that area. It doesn't help when you are told that your prognosis is that you are and will become worse etc. The group I subscribe to in the U.S, Parkinson's Recovery whom I mentioned earlier has a far more positive outlook, they are the sort of people that I like to be surrounded with.

Many of you as I mentioned before will be familiar with the Atypical Parkinson's (PSP) Progressive Supra Nuclear Palsy. It is like a Parkinson's plus! My neurologist has been insisting for some years now that this is what he believes I have. I have had two second opinions, which have both refuted it, however he keeps telling me this each time I see him. I don't believe that I have and keep telling him this. I find it really unsettling and depressing, especially when you are trying to maintain a positive attitude.

I find it really difficult to gauge how the PD is progressing. My walking is extremely slow, although I am trying to consciously count and talk to myself as I go. I've always been a talker so am pretty good at conversing with myself. I try to do a short walk most mornings, it is something which I really enjoy, especially as we are fortunate to live close to the river, it is like an early morning meditation.

My breathing continues to be very trying at times, especially when my Madopar is wearing off, and then in that hour or so whilst it is kicking in. I am quite unsteady on my feet, and tend to fall backwards, so have had several falls, fortunately no real damage, apart from pride and some lovely colourful bruises. The worst one was when I fell in the car park, this time tripped over a bollard, so fell forward fracturing my cheekbone and necessitating some sutures inside my mouth.

At times I have feelings of sheer frustration, times when I cannot do my shoes up, rise from a chair, when my feet feel like bricks and I can't lift them to dress in skirts, tights etc. These are just a few of the little daily inconveniences. I sleep very poorly, although of late I have been working hard to improve that. By the end of the day I feel quite fatigued, but I need to remind myself that I am now 77 years of age, and other folk of my age who do not have PD complain of also having sleeping and weariness problems. It is so easy to make PD the culprit for every ache and pain that appears.

For quite a few years I would try to hide my PD, almost as if ashamed of it. Perhaps you may at times have felt the same. I would continually be making excuses for my awkward rising from the chair in the hairdressing salon, for my stiffness when walking etc. I have now overcome that and find that being honest and upfront is the way to go. People once they know are always empathetic.
I am reminded as I write this of making a phone call to my brother all those years ago to tell him what my diagnosis was. Understandably I was upset. I will always remember his response. He said, " Just remember you are who you have always been, this makes no difference." Wise words - we are not defined by our disease.

I have never wanted to have PD, nobody would!! It is debilitating, and quite unpredictable. I find that no two days are the same. Sometimes I try to figure this out, however often it appears that there is no rhyme or reason. Little things keep happening. I have trouble now swallowing my pills. It is very difficult to initiate the swallowing action, I find putting something else in my mouth at the same time (not protein of course) helps overcome this. Climbing into bed and somehow getting comfortable is not easy. Depending where I am in my medication cycle determines whether I need help to lift my legs out of the car if we have been shopping etc. Sometimes I find myself in tears at the frustration of it all.

Having said that having this illness has brought lovely people into my life whom I would probably never have met. Folk like my Bowen therapist, who believes in me, who is totally positive, and shares much laughter and fun. I am so fortunate to be surrounded by friends and family who are constantly affirming me. The American activist and poet Dr. Maya Angelou whom I have been reading lately, in one of her quotes speaks about how when there are dark clouds, we can be a rainbow. I am thankful to all my dear friends who have been the rainbows in my dark cloud.

This year my husband and I are not travelling to the UK. I find the airport walking is very trying, also the flight itself is not easy for a body that gets stiff so easily. I could have a wheel chair to traverse the distance as I have had in the last couple of years. It is a great service, however it is my vanity which gets in the way - the same applies when someone mentions a walker or a stick. Somehow I feel defeated at the thought, I would prefer to leave these aids until I have no choice. Instead we are trying a cruise, which does away with all the complexities of air travel.

On the whole I find that just as I knew so very little before I actually had this disease, that most lay people do not know a lot about PD. Most associate it with tremor, which I don't have, for which I am thankful. I am very sad when I hear of people who are given the diagnosis, which is almost to them a death sentence, a dying to the life they once had! This is so wrong. We all need hope, if we take that away, what do we have left. I have heard many PD people speaking or writing on this very thing whose outlook is so positive. They do not say, "I have Parkinson's disease". However instead say something like " I experience some symptoms" which happen to be called that. They do not focus on the fact that they have been told that it is degenerative, however rather on the positive things that can be done to help overcome the symptoms. That is how I want to be.

I guess it is like sailing on uncharted waters. We never know how high the waves are going to be or what might lie beneath, however as I use this analogy I am reminded that life is rather like that with or without PD. I remember last Easter day waking up to a grey and miserable morning. When I complained how depressing it was I was reminded that high above the clouds the sun was still shinning. I pray that I will remember when the day may be difficult, that the sun will shine again.

PART 2 MY JOURNEY WITH PARKINSON'S 2016

I recently read this little quote, *"If you keep looking back on your yesterdays, you are not living in the gift that the present is!"*

As I write this I am trying to be mindful of this little bit of wisdom. I am trying to live in the moment however with PD it is not the easiest thing to do.

Since I last put pen to paper, (or perhaps I should say fingers to keys or whatever the relevant digital equivalent), I seem to be having more of a struggle coping with the day-to-day happenings.
I realise this is obviously because in the last eighteen months or so my PD has become worse and I have needed to adjust my medication accordingly.

Lately I have been giving thought to this new situation and trying to work out some new strategies, which might help me to cope. There are some days when I wonder why I am bothering, after all it would be far easier to sit in a corner and feel sorry for myself. Happily these days are few and far between, mostly when my whole body seems to be rebelling, painful knees which both need replacing, stiff neck and aching arm. The days when I seem to be trying to find enough hot packs to accommodate these miserable things, not to mention my breathing difficulties, which I experience on a daily basis.

I probably sound as if I'm having a real. "Poor me day!" And I guess in a way I am. Poor is not a good word to use, as I am rich in so many ways. Rich in great friendships, people who support me, who encourage in all sorts of ways. It seems that whenever it is needed I will have a phone call, a visit and quite often an email, which will lift me up, putting things into perspective again. I am also, as mentioned in my earlier writing so aware and thankful for the many folk who pray for me.

Just recently a well-meaning friend said to me, God only gives these trials to those whom He knows are strong enough to carry them! How often have we heard that quoted or perhaps a similar train of thought? As I reflected on this statement I realised that this was not the God I know. My God is a loving Father who wants only the best for me. Could I believe that the God who has counted every hair on my head and holds me in the palm of his hand could give me this complex and cruel disease? Would a loving earthly father do this to his child? Of course not! So there is no way our "Father in Heaven" would do it. I guess this comes back to the vexing question of suffering, which is something I am quite happy to leave in my mystery box. It may be simplistic but I believe that we live in a fallen world and that God sheds as many tears as we do as he sees our pain and suffering.

I am reminded of that lovely verse in the psalms where David is in a lot of danger and he calls out to God to keep his tears in a bottle. Wonderful imagery! I remember someone once explaining that there was a legend from antiquity which spoke about the warriors of old who when going off to battle would leave the bottle to gather the tears of sadness of their sweethearts! When they arrived home their loved one would present them with the bottle as a token and memory of their love for them.

What a lovely illustration this is for us, in this metaphor it is reversed. It is God who is shedding his tears over our suffering, in the times of grief, loss, and ill health when for one reason or another we have experienced sadness. He is saying to us "You really matter to me, I care so much, I am with you in your times of sadness." He is keeping His tears for us in His bottle.

When next we shed tears (and these days I seem to shed many) perhaps we can recall this lovely picture and know that we are not alone, I like to think that perhaps some day in Heaven we will find a bottle with our name on full of those very same tears.

There are things in this life that we will never know the answer to no matter how long and hard we may try. I often think especially now that I have grown older and the years left are diminishing of all the time that is spent in deep theological discussion, in religious arguing etc which, perhaps could have been spent more meaningfully.

These days I look around at all my possessions and my mind turns to decluttering. I know I am not alone in this, many of my friends of similar ages are on the same path. We have reached the stage in our life when we realise we have far too much "stuff". As I write this I am convicted that sometimes we need to declutter our mind as well. Thinking along these lines I know that this is a process which for me has been happening over time, probably a natural progression as the years have passed and I am now facing old age. It sounds strange actually writing those words "old age". Are you like me? I really never thought I would grow old and somehow, here I am... it has happened...and strangely enough even with this PD which affects my body in all sorts of ways I still do not feel old.

The decluttering of our mind can be a liberating experience. For me it has resulted in more tolerance in many areas, fixed ideas which were hangovers from younger days have been replaced with more understanding and a willingness for greater listening. We are all products of our time our upbringing etc. and change if necessary is always possible.

One of the other subjects that I have consigned to my mystery box is the healing power of our God. If you are like me you also may have spent time pondering on the efficacy of prayer. Why do we pray for our healing, what happens when so many friends are praying for you and yet no answers seem to be forthcoming? Do we stop believing? Do we stop praying?

Some years ago when travelling in the UK we found ourselves in Salisbury, we had visited the Cathedral when we had spent a couple of years living there in the early '60's. So here we were again spending time in this beautiful place. It was very late in the day and the evening service was just about to begin, so we joined in the service of worship which led into their monthly healing service. The next morning we went down town and picked up a couple of books from the local charity shop to read on the flight home.

One book in particular I had not paid much attention to, we were now home and I had the opportunity to read. What a wonderful story. It recounted the healing of Dorothy Kerin. Dorothy was miraculously healed by God in her early 20's. I read it and reread it, then lent it to one of my praying friends, who asked me had I thought of checking out the healing centre that Dorothy had established. Perhaps it was still there? This I did! And the rest is history.

From then on each year when we travelled to the UK to visit friends we would visit this beautiful centre at Groomsbridge in Sussex. This is so beautiful that it is hard to put into words. You feel the peace of God stealing over you even as you drive along the lovely entrance drive. It is now a hospital as well, which is dedicated to wholeness and healing. The chapel of Christ the Healer which Dorothy had built is a place of blessing where Healing services are held twice a week. You might ask with all those visits, "Were you not healed?" My answer is yes and no! I still have my PD, but healing comes in many ways. As I sat in that lovely chapel the sense of the presence of God's Spirit there with me was very real. That was enough.

To add a postscript to this, I remember reading an article on prayer many years ago by Madelaine L'Engle one of my favourite writers. At present one of her very popular books. " A Wrinkle In Time", is showing in the cinemas. Madelaine writes and I quote,

> *" We only know that in this life sometimes prayers are magnificently answered. Surely the prayers have sustained me and are sustaining me. Perhaps there will be unexpected answers to some prayers, answers I may*

> *not be aware of for years. But they are not wasted, they are not lost. I do not know where they have gone, but I believe that God holds them, hands outstretched to receive them like precious pearls."*

In the intervening time since I last wrote there have been happenings some of which were not really what I would have chosen. The one which affected me most was falling in the kitchen last August and fracturing the top of my humerus and impacting the shoulder. It was a bad break, was misaligned and because of my PD and my symptom of breathing difficulties it was decided that the surgery was out of the question. I spent two weeks in hospital getting the pain under control and then home under the care of a transition care team organised by the hospital.

My time in hospital, although I was looked after very well and generally speaking found the nursing staff very kind I found myself with a great deal of frustration. I am including this, as perhaps it has been the experience of you who may be reading this? Or may be something that you may recall if you also find yourself in a similar situation. As a rule, when you are admitted to the ward your present medications are taken and placed in a safe place to be dispensed at a relevant time by the staff. That may be fine with the majority of meds, which are taken on a regular and fairly predictable basis. The problem with folk who have PD is that they may vary from day to day, even from hour to hour.

As my major symptom is my difficulty with extreme shortness of breath I often continue my meds through the night, often every three hours ...although that varies depending on the quality of my sleep, I never wake myself to take any pills, however if I do wake and am having trouble with my breathing I will need to take a pill. This of course means my daytime regime is governed by the times I have medicated through the night.

When in hospital although I tried to explain this it really fell on deaf ears. One nurse even said, "I have nursed other PD patients and they have their meds four times a day". Consequently they would check their charts to see when I last had it and would bring it four hours later. I spoke to the physician who was looking after me and asked him to explain the situation to the staff. Things improved slightly, however finally I gave up! My husband brought me in another bottle of pills and I medicated myself. When they brought my meds I would accept them and keep them for another day. I later spoke to my neurologist about this - he was sympathetic and said that he had had similar problems with other patients. He said that the nursing staff generally speaking did not have training in the treatment of PD patients. If I find myself in hospital again, I will make sure I have a relevant letter from my Neurologist explaining the dosage of my meds.

On leaving hospital I was introduced as I mentioned above to the transition care team. This was a service that we did not know existed, however we could not speak highly enough of the care. If you are reading this and do not know of the availability of this service, it is worth your while to tuck it away in your mind for another day. Hopefully you will not need it, however as we have found the future is full of unknowns!

For the first three months every morning a helper came to assist me with showering and dressing. This was very helpful as being my right arm and combining with the unsteadiness of the PD, it certainly made things easier and safer. Also they provided a case manager, Physiotherapist, Occupational therapist all who provided the necessary information about appliances in the house such as grab rails etc., also making sure I had the exercises that I needed to facilitate healing my arm.

I really did enjoy and appreciate these very kind women, however I have to say that at that time I lost all my modesty, dignity etc. (whatever you like to call it.) I know I am not alone with these feelings and I am sure that many of you will identify with what I am saying. I guess it is a fact of life, as we grow older most of us are going to need some sort of help.

Sometimes we need to swallow our pride and accept this new stage in our life. I think they found me very stubborn! They came armed with walking sticks, walkers etc., all of which I refused to have. For all these years one of the ways that I have been dealing with this Disease is to try to be as positive as possible. I feel that once I give in I will be sacrificing a little more of my independence. I just hope that when the time comes when I do need to embrace aids of some description that I will have the common sense to recognise it.

My arm healed well even though I did not have the surgery. As I write this it is seven months later and I have a good range of movement, although in certain positions it can be quite painful and still I cannot put any strain on it to help me rise from chairs etc. Speaking of rising from chairs, bed etc, this is becoming far more difficult as is my propensity to fall. Most of my falling seems to occur in the bedroom, dressing, undressing etc. My falling is always backwards, so I try to do some exercises to help this problem.

These days my voice is a constant concern, at times it is almost impossible to have a decent conversation. Not only is my voice extremely soft, however a lot of the time it takes a real effort for me to speak. I no longer enjoy being with groups of people nearly as much as I once did for this very reason. I always have been a great talker and like nothing better than to sit down and have a good chat.

I have gone back to my speech pathologist, however probably should be more diligent with my speech exercises. For the last year I have not had my Bowen therapy as sadly my lovely therapist suffered a stroke and was no longer able to continue. I am intending to find another therapist in the near future.

My meds have increased and I am needing to take them more frequently. I also have found a new Movement Disorder Neurologist, whom I have seen twice and who seems to understand my present needs. I am still chewing gum, which I don't particularly like however it does help me with my dry mouth and also the swallowing of excess saliva etc.

I am very aware of how easy it is when one suffers with PD to become anti-social. It is so easy to make excuses for not doing something or going somewhere. I recall some years ago a speech pathologist saying to me how important it was to keep talking even if it was difficult. She went on to say how many folk gave up because of the difficulty and refused to go out. (A case for if you don't use it you lose it!) If you are reading this and you have PD you will readily identify with it. Even writing about it rather depresses me. It is not only the talking, however the very fact of changing your clothes etc to go somewhere can become a real chore, especially if you are unsteady on your feet as I often am.

I have to be careful what I wear, as a lot of clothes, particularly since I had my arm injury, are not the easiest to get out of, fortunately my husband is mostly here when I need to undress, however if he wasn't I would have to be far more selective about what I would choose to wear.

For those of us who have husbands or partners this can also put a strain on relationships. Even the steadiest and happiest marriage can suffer when one partner has a chronic illness. I have a very patient husband, however at times we both become frustrated with our situation. My voice is soft, sometimes almost non-existent and his hearing is not exactly the sharpest. (Not that he would admit to that). I speak, he does not hear, I am constantly repeating myself which I find very tiring at times. You can imagine the way our conversation goes, each one blaming the other for not hearing, not speaking loudly enough etc.

Even when you live with someone and they see how your illness affects you, it is still not easy for them to understand how you really feel. I used to in pre PD days love the early morning. I would wake up early full of energy and ready to go. These days I usually have a couple of doses of my meds before I am steady enough to face having my shower etc.

We used to travel a lot, something which my husband loves doing. To me now the thought of it makes me feel weary, yet I am really unable to explain adequately my objections to travelling. I do very little housework as bending over is an invitation to fall. So I am happy to have someone coming in to do the heavier chores, while I am OK with dusting etc.

I love cooking, and I still cook a lot. These days my cooking happens at odd times, mostly when my breathing is OK, and I am feeling relatively normal. I still love entertaining which we have done much of over our lifetime. Our family is very helpful and if I want to have people in for a dinner party, I will do all the cooking and they will come and help with the serving and cleaning up. When I broke my arm my family were incredibly helpful. My freezer was always full of meals etc and they were here on a regular basis, I am incredibly blessed with my husband and children.

Life is special, sometimes we have some hard bumps that come our way, however we are not dismayed...we have been given a great gift, the beauty of the original wrapping may have somewhat faded. As we peel the layers away, we may find the colours more enduring! We will keep unwrapping!

All profits from this book are to be donated to Parkinson's Queensland Inc.

ACKNOWLEDGEMENTS

With love and thanks to my caring family who have helped in many ways... from cooking to correcting, and above all together with many supportive friends have encouraged me when I doubted my own ability.

To my lovely daughter-in-law Mika who has been responsible for all the illustrations and to Dana who has edited and made it all possible.

I love and appreciate you.

Kay

www.ingramcontent.com/pod-product-compliance
Lightning Source LLC
Chambersburg PA
CBHW042129160426
43198CB00022B/2957